SUPERPOWER LIFE SKILLS FOR TEENS WITH AMBITION

HOW TO MASTER RESILIENCE, CONFLICT RESOLUTION, TEAMWORK, MONEY MANAGEMENT, CRITICAL THINKING, AND MORE TO BECOME YOUR BEST SELF

MIKE KLAASSEN

Paperback edition ISBN: 9798990628649
eBook edition ISBN: 9798990628656
Hardcover edition ISBN: 9798990628663

ACKNOWLEDGMENTS

I thank my wife, Gerri, for her loving support and encouragement, which made this book possible. Thanks to my friends Heather Harrison and Holly Harper for providing early draft readings. I also appreciate the encouragement and support of my friend and fellow author, L. D. Alford.

Dedicated to the ambitious teenagers who will shape the future of our world in so many wonderful ways.

CONTENTS

AMBITION

Ambition is an internal force characterized by a strong desire, determination, or drive to achieve success, reach goals, or fulfill a vision, often beyond one's current status or achievements. It involves setting high aspirations, pursuing them with tenacity, and being willing to overcome obstacles and challenges along the way.[1] Ambition can come into play in various aspects of life, such as career, education, personal development, or any field in which one aims to excel.

Ambitious individuals are typically goal-oriented, focused, and motivated by a sense of purpose. They possess a forward-thinking mindset and continuously seek opportunities for growth and improvement. Ambition is not merely about achieving external markers of success, such as wealth, status, or power—it also encompasses personal satisfaction, fulfillment, and realizing one's potential.[2]

Ambition drives people to push their limits and strive for their best. When balanced with other values such as integrity, compassion, and cooperation, ambition enriches the journey toward personal achievements, aligning one's quest for success with ethical considerations and a positive impact on society.[3]

In essence, ambition is a key ingredient for personal and professional development, driving individuals to set goals, work toward them with dedication, and continually seek to elevate their standards of achievement and success.

INTRODUCTION

This may be one of the most important books you'll ever read, but it comes with a note of caution. You probably have already considered this, but if you don't like being teased or ridiculed, you may want to avoid reading about ambition and superpowers while you're in the presence of others. Not everybody wants you to achieve your dreams, especially if those people feel that makes them look bad. Sadly, that can include friends and family. I encourage you to read this book when you have a bit of privacy; you know, like you would a book about something very personal, such as sex education. If you must, put this book somewhere safe until you're ready to learn how to achieve your wildest dreams.

Welcome back!

If you're like me, some of your earliest memories include watching a man in a red cape fly at supersonic speeds, bend steel bars with his bare hands, and see with X-ray vision. Fantastic superheroes are part of our culture, which means they're part of us as individuals. This book is also about a superhero—the superhero you will become—not by leaping tall buildings or swinging from skyscrapers, but by mastering the art of life itself.

Imagine waking up every day with a sense of purpose, excitement, and confidence in your ability to tackle whatever challenges come your way. This book isn't just about surviving the teen years—it's about thriving and setting the stage for a life filled with achievement and fulfillment. Here, you'll discover practical strategies and empowering insights to master essential life skills like habit management, emotional intelligence, and leadership. Whether you're aiming for academic excellence, personal growth, or future career success, this book is your roadmap to becoming the superhero of your own life story.

You may be facing a tumultuous phase of life when identity crises, mental health challenges, and the overwhelming pressure of digital communication threaten to define you. The teenage years have become more challenging in today's fast-paced, hyper-connected world.[1]

Statistics paint a troubling picture. Many teenagers experience some form of mental health issue, with anxiety and depression being the most common.[2] The prevalence of cyberbullying is on the rise as the online world becomes an inescapable source of both validation and torment.[3] Amidst this storm of emotions, teenagers strive to find their footing, balancing the demands of education, relationships, and familial expectations.

This book offers the tools and understanding to navigate and overcome these adversities. As a proud father and grandfather, I've been blessed with a wonderful life full of challenges and rewards that gave me insights through experience. I'm committed to sharing whatever I can to empower you toward a life of fulfillment and achievement. We'll embark on a journey together, exploring essential life skills that promise to transform your formative years from a time of turmoil into an era of growth and self-empowerment.

With the help of some of my favorite superheroes as examples (including Spider-Man, Wonder Woman, and Cyborg), you'll learn to tackle the challenges of adolescence confidently, equipped with the ability to make informed decisions, forge meaningful connections, and foster a positive outlook on life. This guide aims to unlock your inherent potential and encourage you to embrace your unique capabilities.

The Power of Life Skills

Strategic life skills, which I call superpowers, are the cornerstones of both personal and professional success, extending beyond academic achievements to encompass the real-world competencies that enable effective navigation of life's complexities.

Addressed within these pages is a portfolio of strategic life skills in seven categories:

- Holistic Well-Being
- Core Personal Development
- Analytical and Decision-Making Skills
- Communication and Interpersonal Skills[4]
- Leadership and Teamwork
- Practical Life Management
- Technology and Learning Skills[5]

Why Bother Learning These Skills Now?

You may wonder if one book can address such a wide range of topics with enough depth to make a difference in your life. Or maybe you feel you're too young to be concerned about strategic competencies. This book isn't about transforming you into an overnight expert—it's about establishing a foundation for lifelong learning and growth. The goal is to provide enough insight to offer immediate benefits while setting you on a path to deeper exploration.

Finding What You Need

Another valid question is whether you could learn everything you need about these skills from other sources. Of course, you can—a vast pool of knowledge is available through libraries, bookstores, and the Internet. What this book does, like no other, is distill the information and organize it into a cohesive framework, potentially saving you enormous time and effort while giving you a head start in putting these skills to work.

This book includes a lot of material, which may be intimidating to some readers. Not to worry—recall words attributed to South African leader Desmond Tutu: "There's only one way to eat an elephant—one bite at a time."[6] Don't feel like you have to rush through the book from cover to cover. A good strategy is to read one superpower at a time, then pause to reflect on that information, letting your mind organize and assimilate it. If you have a particular interest or issue to deal with, look at the table of contents or thumb through the index to locate that specific subject. Later, this book may also be a handy desk reference for addressing issues as they arise. The various chapters and superpowers may also inspire presentations in class, clubs, and workshops, creating opportunities to reinforce what you've learned and expand your knowledge with further research.

Can a Book Really Change Your Life?

You may wonder if reading a single book can alter the trajectory of your life. I assure you that it can. When I was a sophomore in high school, I read a book that changed my life almost immediately, and I continue to build on that foundation to this day. Some of the information in that book is addressed in this one, but it represents a tiny fraction of the information presented here. I'll always be thankful that that book was available to me as a teen, but this is the book I wish I had available at your age. I hope someday, decades into the future, you'll be able to reflect on how this book improved the quality of your life.

Change Takes Time

A reality check is appropriate—changing your personal behavior, habits, and routines can be challenging. You may find some changes easy—you decide to make a change and then stick with it. Congratulations when that happens, but please don't get discouraged if some changes require multiple attempts over an extended period. Even the most minor changes can take some effort and persistence. Instead of making multiple changes simultaneously, which can lead to frustration or defeat, focusing on one change at a time is often more effective. Gradually, small steps can build upon each other, leading to significant improvement.

Recognize Your Progress

As you read this book, you may notice that you're already doing some of the recommended practices and already have some of the skills described. That shows your home life, education, and extracurricular activities are paying off—you're already on the journey of developing your strategic life skills! You'll probably also notice changes you decide to implement as soon as possible while you're still a teenager. Go for it! You'll also realize that some aspects of these superpower life skills will likely take years, even decades, to master. Embrace those as part of your life mission.

A Hero's Journey

This path is not one of ease and shortcuts. True transformation demands perseverance and a willingness to face setbacks head-on. Each step forward in mastering these competencies is a stride toward realizing your aspirations. Recall the *Star Wars* journey of Luke Skywalker, who, after initial skepticism about The Force within him, grew to become a master Jedi through years of effort. This book is an invitation to a similar adventure of self-discovery and mastery.

As we delve into these superpower life skills, remember that this journey is not about becoming someone else—it's about becoming the best version of yourself. Each skill we explore will build upon the last, intertwining and amplifying your abilities to shape a future that is uniquely yours.

Are you ready to explore the depths of your potential and emerge as the hero of your own story? Turn the page, and let's embark on this transformation together, unlocking the extraordinary potential within you.

HOLISTIC WELL-BEING

Holistic *well-being* refers to a balanced state of health that encompasses not just the physical but also the mental and emotional dimensions of life. It involves taking care of your body through proper nutrition, exercise, and sleep while also nurturing your mind and emotions. Holistic well-being recognizes that all these areas are interconnected, and achieving harmony contributes to an overall sense of balance and fulfillment.[1]

Imagine Batman, who, after a night of outwitting villains and safeguarding the city, still dedicates time to physical training and mindfulness.[2] This iconic superhero understands the importance of holistic well-being—balancing the intense stress of crimefighting with personal health and mental clarity. The superhuman ability to manage stress, maintain peak physical condition, and stay mentally sharp is not just for the comics—it's a model of self-care and resilience that you, too, can master.

This chapter is about mastering stress management, wellness management, self-reflection, and mindfulness—essential life skills for thriving in today's fast-paced world. As we explore these superpowers, remember that this journey is uniquely yours. There's no one-size-fits-all approach to holistic well-being— different strategies may work better for you than others, and that's okay. Consider all the ideas and select those that make the most sense for you. By engaging with the ideas and practices presented here, you can become the architect of your own well-being—to create a life of balance, health, and fulfillment.

Let's begin our journey by exploring the superpower of stress management.

SUPERPOWER #1: STRESS MANAGEMENT

Stress management is the ability to recognize, control, and reduce the impact of stress on your mind and body. It involves understanding the sources of stress, identifying how it affects you physically and emotionally, and applying various techniques to manage those effects.[3]

Unfortunately, we now live in a world where stress is accepted as a normal part of life. The odd moment of stress can actually be good for you because it can motivate you to get things done. However, chronic or ongoing stress can wreak havoc on your mental and physical health. You may have noticed that you're struggling to sleep, you have tension in your muscles, or you're getting more headaches.[4]

Research shows that when teens are under intense amounts of stress, more cortisol (the stress hormone) is released in the body, which can increase heart rate and blood pressure.[5] Mentally, constant stress can increase your risk of anxiety and depression.[6]

The Powers of Stress Management

Mastering stress management can profoundly improve your life in many ways. By managing stress effectively, you clear away mental clutter, allowing for sharper focus, sound decision-making, and more creative thinking. Rather than being overwhelmed by tasks, you'll be able to approach them calmly and confidently, leading to greater productivity and success. Stress management also has a significant impact on your physical health, as prolonged stress can lead to issues like heart disease and a weakened immune system.

Emotionally, mastering stress management builds resilience—the ability to recover from setbacks and face adversity with a calm perspective. With these tools at your disposal, you can handle life's challenges more effectively. Stress management also strengthens relationships by reducing tension and conflict. Effectively managing stress enables you to communicate more openly, resolve conflicts constructively, and provide genuine support, fostering more profound and harmonious relationships with others.

Finally, mastering stress allows you to reclaim control over your life. Instead of being reactive, you can navigate life's ups and downs with a sense of inner peace and contentment. You'll find that managing stress not only makes you healthier but also happier, as you cultivate a sense of fulfillment and joy even in the face of life's challenges. Incorporating this superpower into your daily routine equips you to thrive, paving the way for a more successful and balanced future.[7]

Strategies for Specific Sources of Stress

Identifying the types and causes of stress is the first step toward managing them. Here are some potential stressors and strategies for addressing them.

- **Academic stress.** Balance your schedule, prioritize tasks, break them into manageable steps, and ask for help from teachers or tutors if needed.
- **Social stress.** Surround yourself with supportive friends, communicate openly, and set boundaries to maintain healthy interactions. Don't spend time with people who bring you down.
- **Body image.** Avoid the temptation to compare yourself to others, especially when looking at images on TV, in movies, or online. Instead, focus on what you can control—nurturing your well-being, embracing your unique self, and pursuing a balanced, healthy lifestyle—rather than striving to meet someone else's standards.[8]
- **Family disagreements.** Engage in respectful communication with family members and seek support from a trusted adult or counselor. Remember that you don't always have to agree with each other, but you should respect that everyone is entitled to their own beliefs.
- **Significant life changes.** Practice self-care, maintain a routine, and consider joining support groups. There are many online support groups for specific life changes, and sometimes it's reassuring to see how others handle these stressors.[9]

Learning how to manage these specific sources of stress now can give you a head start on adulthood as well as improve your teen years.

How to Wield Stress Management

Like Batman, who faces constant challenges and high-stress situations in Gotham, you, too, can master the ability to manage stress by following this step-by-step process.

1. **Awareness.** Identify the situations, people, or tasks that trigger stress. By recognizing your stressors, you can manage them more effectively.
2. **Deep, slow breaths.** Deep breathing activates your parasympathetic nervous system, the opposite of the fight-or-flight response.[10] Whenever you feel overwhelmed, pause, breathe deeply, and center yourself.
3. **Time management.** Effective time management reduces stress and increases productivity. Create a schedule or to-do list that prioritizes tasks and allows time for work and relaxation. Break larger tasks into smaller steps and tackle them one at a time.
4. **One thing at a time.** You might think that multitasking gets more done quickly, but your brain struggles to switch from one task to the next and you may find yourself making more mistakes. Focus on one task at a time.[11]
5. **Self-care.** Engage in activities that nourish your body, mind, and soul. Whether it's taking a hot bath, walking in nature, or spending time with loved ones, make self-care a priority.
6. **Seek support.** When overwhelmed by stress, reach out for support. Talk to a trusted friend, family member, or mentor, and consider professional help. Surround yourself with a supportive network. [12]
7. **Adapt and adjust.** Be willing to adapt and adjust your approach as needed. Explore new techniques and strategies for managing stress. With practice, develop a personalized toolkit of stress management techniques.[13]

Just like Batman's ability to stay calm under pressure, you can learn to manage stress by identifying your triggers and using techniques to stay focused. Batman doesn't panic when faced with overwhelming threats—instead, he applies strategies like deep breathing and staying composed to think clearly and act decisively in high-stakes situations. You can develop similar control over your stress.

Training Missions to Develop This Superpower

This training mission requires you to follow the 4As: avoid, alter, adapt, and accept.[14]

- **Avoid any unnecessary stress.** If there are conversation topics that stress you out, don't engage in them—this includes topics that you find distressing on the news or social media. Learn how to say no to things that you don't want to do so that you can protect your time and energy.
- **Alter the situation.** When you strongly disagree with something, speak up in an assertive way and express your feelings. For example, if a friend is making racist comments that make you feel uncomfortable or angry, let them know.
- **Adapt to the stressor.** Perfection isn't always necessary. Consider how often you've tweaked a project, hoping to improve it, only to end up with no real difference. Sometimes, a more balanced approach—compromising and finding a middle ground—can be the key to easing stress rather than battling against it.
- **Accept the things you can't change.** There's no point stressing about the things you can't control. Some examples of what you can't control are the thoughts, opinions, and actions of others. You also can't control what has happened in the past—now is the time to forgive, whether that's yourself or others.[15]

In the 2012 film *The Dark Knight Rises*, Bruce Wayne (Batman) faces immense pressure as Gotham descends into chaos under Bane's control. Despite being physically broken and imprisoned, Bruce remains composed, methodically planning his return. His exceptional stress management is evident when he escapes the prison, regains his physical strength, and devises a strategy to defeat Bane. This illustrates how Batman stays calm and focused, using resilience and mental discipline to manage extreme stress and push forward in the face of overwhelming adversity.[16]

Action Items

- Before you read any further, take a moment to identify the types and causes of stress in your life.
- For each stressor in your life, consider how you're currently managing that stress. Take pride in the progress you've already achieved in developing this superpower.
- For each stressor in your life, evaluate the effectiveness of your current strategy to manage that stress.
- If you decide that one or more of your current strategies for managing stress need to be improved, consider at least one to implement.
- Develop a plan for implementing that improvement.

Now that we've addressed stress management, let's move on to the superpower life skill of wellness management.

SUPERPOWER #2: WELLNESS MANAGEMENT

Wellness management is the ability to maintain a balanced and healthy lifestyle by focusing on diet, exercise, and sleep. Together, these three elements form the foundation of a well-rounded approach to physical and mental well-being.

The Powers of Wellness Management

Wellness management is your superpower for maintaining balance in your body and mind. By eating nutritious foods, you fuel your body with the energy it needs to stay sharp and active throughout the day. Regular exercise strengthens your muscles and boosts your mood, helping you handle stress with ease. And getting enough sleep? That's like recharging your personal battery, so you wake up focused and ready to tackle any challenges. Mastering wellness management means feeling healthier, thinking clearer, and having the energy to chase your goals—every day.

Batman knows the importance of maintaining peak physical condition through consistent training, balanced nutrition, and prioritizing rest. To perform at his best, he fuels his body with the right nutrients, engages in rigorous workouts, and ensures he's rested and ready for action. Following Batman's example, your wellness management can power your daily energy, focus, and overall well-being.[17]

Eating Nutritious Food

Consuming the right nutrients is essential for unlocking your superpowers. Think of your body as a high-performance machine needing premium fuel. Eating nutritious food can significantly improve your life in multiple ways. A diet rich in essential nutrients like omega-3 fatty acids,[18] antioxidants,[19] and vitamins helps boost brain function by enhancing memory, concentration, and cognitive abilities. With fruits, vegetables, lean proteins, and whole grains, you'll fuel your brain to perform at its best, helping you think strategically and stay sharp.[20]

Eating well also boosts your energy levels. By providing your body with a balanced mix of carbohydrates, proteins, and fats, you can maintain a steady supply of energy throughout the day, avoiding the crashes that come from sugary snacks and processed foods.[21] Additionally, a nutritious diet positively affects your mood and mental health. Certain foods can increase serotonin levels, which help promote happiness and well-being while reducing the effects of stress, anxiety, and depression.[22]

Good nutrition strengthens your immune system as well, making you less vulnerable to illnesses. Antioxidant-rich foods, along with essential vitamins and minerals, provide your body with the defenses it needs to fight off infections.[23] On a physical level, a balanced diet improves your fitness and endurance by providing the necessary nutrients like protein for muscle repair and growth,[24] and calcium and iron to keep your bones strong.[25]

In the long run, consistently eating nutritious foods can reduce your risk of chronic diseases like obesity, type 2 diabetes, heart disease, and certain cancers. By making healthy eating a priority, you create the foundation for a more vibrant and healthier life.[26]

The Skinny on Fats

When it comes to dietary fats, the Mayo Clinic[27] explains that there are two primary categories: saturated fats and unsaturated fats, which are further divided into monounsaturated fats and polyunsaturated fats. Each type affects our bodies differently, and most foods contain a blend of these fats. While some fats are essential for healthy cell function, others can increase the risk of disease. So, how do we know which fats to include in our diet and which to limit?

The Mayo Clinic offers these straightforward tips for making healthier choices about fats.

- **Opt for plant-based oils.** Instead of using butter or lard, try sautéing vegetables with olive oil. For high-heat cooking like stir-frying or searing, canola oil is a good choice.
- **Incorporate fish into your diet.** Especially oily fish like salmon, which is rich in heart-healthy omega-3 fatty acids.
- **Choose lean meats and skinless poultry.** Trim visible fat from cuts of meat and remove skin from poultry to reduce saturated fat intake.
- **Go for low-fat dairy products.** Swap full-fat options for lower-fat alternatives in milk, yogurt, and cheese.
- **Snack smart with whole fruits and vegetables.** They're filling, nutritious, and naturally low in unhealthy fats.
- **Limit processed foods.** Many are packed with unhealthy saturated fats, so choose fresh options whenever possible.
- **Read labels carefully.** Even low-fat or fat-free processed foods can be loaded with added sugars and sodium, so checking the nutrition information is important.

By making these small adjustments, you can enjoy the benefits of healthy fats while controlling less desirable ones. [28]

Tips for a Balanced Diet

- **Drink water.** Stay hydrated by drinking water throughout the day. Add some fruit slices to make things interesting.[29]
- **Eat three meals a day.** Ensure your body gets the energy and nutrients it needs.[30]
- **Include healthy snacks.** Choose fruits, vegetables, nuts, or yogurt instead of starchy or sugary foods.[31]
- **Increase your fiber intake.** Consume whole grains, fruits, vegetables, and legumes.[32]

- **Decrease your salt intake.** Cut back on salty foods and choose low-sodium options.[33]
- **Eat balanced meals.** Mix protein, carbohydrates, and healthy fats in each meal.[34]
- **Choose healthier cooking methods.** Try baking, broiling, or grilling instead of frying.[35]
- **Be mindful of added sugars.** Reduce sugar intake and watch for hidden sugars in snacks and drinks.[36]
- **Eat lean meats.** Opt for lean cuts of meat, including chicken and fish.[37]
- **Prepare your meals.** Learn to prepare simple, healthy meals.[38]

Fueling your body with the right nutrients is essential for unlocking your superpowers. A diet rich in essential nutrients lays the foundation for a healthier, more vibrant life.

Exercising Regularly

Batman doesn't just rely on his gadgets—his physical fitness is a core part of his ability to fight crime. By incorporating exercise into his daily routine, he maintains peak physical condition, much like how you can use regular physical activity to stay energized and focused.

Regular exercise can significantly enhance your life in numerous ways. It boosts brain health by improving cognitive functions such as attention, memory, and problem-solving skills. You'll find that staying active sharpens your focus and mental clarity, helping you perform better in both academic and everyday tasks.[39]

Exercise also plays a key role in managing your weight. By burning calories, increasing your metabolism, and building muscle mass, it helps you maintain a healthy body composition.[40] Beyond weight management, regular exercise reduces your risk of various diseases. It lowers blood pressure, improves cholesterol levels, and decreases the likelihood of developing cardiovascular conditions, type 2 diabetes, and metabolic syndrome.[41]

Strengthening your bones and muscles is another vital benefit of regular exercise. Weight-bearing activities like running and strength training help fortify your bones and build muscle, making you physically stronger and more resilient. In addition, regular exercise enhances your overall fitness, making everyday activities easier to perform and allowing you to tackle physical challenges with greater ease.[42]

By embracing exercise, you improve your physical health, sharpen your mind, and elevate your daily performance.

Tips for Regular Physical Activity

- **Learn simple exercises.** Do bodyweight exercises like lunges, squats, pushups, and hip hinges.[43]
- **Engage in different types of exercise.** Include resistance training, cardio, and high-intensity interval training (HIIT).[44]
- **Commit to sixty minutes of exercise daily.** These may include jogging, swimming, dancing, sports, or brisk walking.[45]
- **Find enjoyable activities.** Make physical activity a sustainable and enjoyable part of your routine.[46]

Increasing Your Physical Activity

There's no need to go overboard and start an exercise regimen that is impossible for you to maintain. You can start with, for example, a 10-minute brisk walk each day and gradually increase the amount of time.[47] Things like taking the stairs instead of the elevator and carrying grocery bags can all help.

Technology is awesome for physical activity. Apps like FitOn are free to join and offer many different types of exercises for different levels and lengths of time. This makes exercising more convenient and easier to incorporate into your daily routine.

To ensure you're taking part in a variety of physical activities, use the following ideas to create a personalized workout that you love.

Aerobic	Muscle Strengthening	Bone Strengthening
Swimming	Sit-ups	Walking
Running	Push-ups	Hiking
Cycling	Squats	Skipping rope
Skating	Pilates	Yoga
Jumping jacks	Rock climbing	Gymnastics
Team sports	Skiing	Volleyball
Dancing	Surfing	Lunges
Boxing	Weightlifting	Tennis

Finally, always make sure you warm up and cool down properly and keep hydrated while you're exercising.

Getting Enough Sleep

Getting enough sleep can enhance your life in multiple ways. Sleep is essential for maintaining physical health, as it allows your body to repair tissues, build muscle, and strengthen the immune system, ensuring that you wake up ready to take on the day. Adequate sleep also sharpens your mental clarity, improving your ability to concentrate, make decisions, and solve problems more effectively.[48]

Emotionally, sleep plays an important role in managing stress and helping you maintain a positive outlook. When well-rested, you're better equipped to handle challenges and stay emotionally balanced.[49] Additionally, sleep boosts creativity, providing your brain with the necessary time to recharge and enabling you to excel in creative pursuits.[50] Establishing a healthy sleep routine not only helps you perform better day-to-day but also sets the foundation for long-term success, allowing you to pursue your ambitions with the energy, clarity, and resilience needed to achieve your goals.

Tips to Improve Sleep

- **Budget enough time for sleep.** Aim for eight to ten hours, even on weekends.
- **Establish a pre-bed routine.** Engage in relaxing activities like reading or mindfulness.
- **Limit caffeine and energy drinks.** Avoid these, especially in the afternoon and evening.

- **Minimize electronic device use.** Such activities may cause mental stimulation that is hard to reverse.[51]
- **Create a sleep-friendly environment.** Keep your bedroom cool, dark, and quiet.
- **Optimize your sleep surface.** Ensure your mattress and pillow are comfortable. Also, don't study in bed—reserve this space for sleeping.
- **Give yourself time to wind down.** Aim for around 30 minutes to chill out before going to bed.
- **Nap with caution.** If you need to take an afternoon nap, try to limit it to no more than 30 minutes.[52]

By following these tips, you can improve the quality of your sleep and overall well-being—and you'll get more out of the time you're awake.

How to Wield This Superpower

Here's a step-by-step process for mastering wellness management.

1. **Self-assessment.** Regularly evaluate your health and well-being.[53]
2. **Goal setting.** Establish clear, achievable health and wellness goals.[54]
3. **Planning.** Develop a structured plan to achieve your goals.
4. **Implementation.** Execute the plan with discipline and motivation.
5. **Monitoring and adjusting.** Track progress and adjust strategies as needed.

Training Missions to Develop This Superpower

Engage in activities such as the following to enhance your wellness-management skills.

- **Nutrition log.** Document what you eat and drink each day for one week.
- **Exercise log.** Document your exercise activities each day for one week.
- **Sleep log.** Document your sleep routine each day for one week.
- **Review and improve.** Formulate an implementation plan based on your logs.

By tracking and analyzing your nutrition, exercise, and sleep habits, you can create a personalized plan that enhances your overall well-being and sets you on a path to optimal health and performance.

In the 2005 film *Batman Begins*, Bruce Wayne demonstrates a deep commitment to both physical and mental wellness after years of intense training. His time with the League of Shadows is marked by disciplined physical conditioning, martial arts mastery, and preparing his body for the challenges ahead. Even after assuming the mantle of Batman, Bruce continues to follow a strict regimen, maintaining peak fitness through rigorous training, proper diet, and rest. This highlights his dedication to wellness management, ensuring his physical health is always at its best to sustain his strength and stamina.[55]

Action Items

- Before you read any further, take a few minutes to review the information presented in this section.
- Imagine yourself decades in the future (after many years of cultivating holistic well-being) and how you use this superpower to achieve your goals.
- Note how you currently address nutrition, exercise, and sleep daily. Take pride in the progress you've already achieved in developing holistic well-being.
- Evaluate the effectiveness of your current nutrition, exercise, and sleep habits in maintaining your wellness.
- If you decide that one or more of your current nutrition, exercise, and sleep practices need to be improved, consider at least one for improvement.
- Develop a plan for implementing that improvement.

Now that we have addressed wellness management, it's time to move on to the superpowers of self-reflection and mindfulness.

SUPERPOWERS #3 & 4: SELF-REFLECTION AND MINDFULNESS

Self-reflection and mindfulness form a powerful duo of strategic life skills. Self-reflection deepens your understanding of who you are,[56] while mindfulness centers you in the present moment, freeing you from worries about the past or future.[57] Since both of these superpowers involve your inner world, they're often mistaken for one another. To make it easier to distinguish between them, I'll explore them together in this chapter. Let's dive into what makes each unique and how they complement one another.

Self-Reflection

Self-reflection is the ability to critically examine your thoughts, actions, and experiences to better understand yourself. It involves taking time to look inward, considering your motivations, strengths, weaknesses, and the impact of your behavior on others. This superpower encourages you to pause and evaluate your past choices, habits, and emotional responses, while also considering how they shape your future decisions and actions. In self-reflection, you develop a more accurate sense of who you are, your values, and what drives your decisions. It requires honesty, introspection, and a willingness to explore your inner world to foster personal growth.[58]

The Powers of Self-Reflection

Unlocking the superpower of self-reflection has the potential to transform multiple aspects of your life. It deepens your self-awareness, allowing you to better understand your thoughts, emotions, and behaviors. This heightened awareness helps you recognize patterns in your actions and reactions, giving you insight into how you navigate different situations. Batman often takes time to reflect on his actions and decisions, analyzing how he can improve in his fight against crime. Self-reflection allows him to continually evolve, just as it can help you grow by evaluating your own choices and learning from your experiences.

Through self-reflection, you develop greater emotional intelligence by learning to understand and manage your emotions more effectively. This skill allows you to navigate relationships and challenges with greater ease. Regular self-reflection helps clarify your values and beliefs, allowing you to identify the guiding principles that shape your decisions and actions.[59]

How to Wield Self-Reflection

Here's a step-by-step process for mastering this superpower.

- **Create a quiet space.** Find a distraction-free place to be alone with your thoughts.
- **Set aside regular time.** Dedicate consistent time for self-reflection.
- **Use a journal.** Write down thoughts and experiences to clarify and record growth.[60]
- **Reflect on your goals.** Evaluate progress and obstacles related to short-term and long-term goals.
- **Analyze your actions and reactions.** Identify patterns and learn more effective ways to handle situations.
- **Practice self-compassion.** Be kind to yourself and view mistakes as learning opportunities.
- **Set actionable steps.** Turn insights into tangible progress with specific actions.
- **Monitor your progress.** Regularly review reflections and actions taken.[61]

Integrating these practices into your routine allows you to cultivate a deeper understanding of yourself and foster continuous personal growth.

Training Missions to Develop Self-Reflection

Engage in activities such as these to enhance this superpower.

- **Engage in creative expression.** Use creative outlets like drawing, music, or writing poetry to explore and understand emotions.

- **Create a vision and goal boards.** Visualize goals and aspirations to clarify intentions and stay motivated.[62]
- **Develop a routine for personal check-ins.** Regularly assess feelings and thoughts to stay connected to your inner self.
- **Reflect on inspirational quotes or books.** Draw insights and motivation from meaningful quotes or passages.
- **Practice gratitude.** Use a journal to think about the things you're thankful for in your life, whether those are relationships or the smaller things, like a meme that makes you laugh.[63]
- **Consider your strengths and weaknesses.** Don't just think about the skills you need to develop. Praise yourself for the things you do well.

In the 2008 film *The Dark Knight*, after the tragic death of Rachel Dawes, Bruce Wayne's childhood friend and love interest, he struggles with the consequences of his choices, especially the impact of his role as Batman on Gotham. Bruce embarks on a deep process of self-reflection, questioning the morality of his actions and the toll his dual life is taking. This inner conflict unfolds in conversations with Alfred, where Bruce voices his doubts and reassesses his motives. These moments of introspection highlight Bruce's capacity for self-reflection as he steps back to evaluate his purpose and the true impact of his actions.[64]

Now that we've explored self-reflection, let's turn to mindfulness.

Mindfulness

Mindfulness is the ability to be fully present and engaged in the current moment, aware of your thoughts, feelings, bodily sensations, and surroundings without judgment or distraction. It involves paying deliberate attention to your experiences as they unfold, allowing you to observe them with clarity and acceptance. This superpower encourages a heightened state of consciousness, where you can focus on the here and now rather than dwelling on the past or worrying about the future. Mindfulness often incorporates practices like deep breathing, mindful observation, and meditation to cultivate calm awareness and intentional living.[65]

The Powers of Mindfulness

Mindfulness is a key part of Batman's approach. In moments of intense focus, whether strategizing his next move or staying grounded in a dangerous situation, Batman demonstrates how important it is to be present in the moment. Practicing mindfulness will help you sharpen your awareness and respond thoughtfully to whatever life throws at you.

Mindfulness improves your emotional regulation by encouraging you to recognize and accept your emotions without reacting impulsively. This creates space for thoughtful responses rather than immediate reactions. Additionally, practicing mindfulness builds resilience by fostering a non-judgmental awareness that allows you to bounce back from setbacks and face challenges more calmly and clearly.[66]

On a physical level, mindfulness is linked to better overall health, with benefits such as lowered blood pressure, improved sleep, and a stronger immune system. By cultivating mindfulness daily, you lay the foundation for a healthier, more balanced, and fulfilling future.[67]

How to Wield Mindfulness

Here's how to effectively use this superpower in your daily life.

1. **Set an intention.** Decide when and where you want to practice mindfulness.
2. **Focus on the present moment.** Whether you're walking, sitting, or lying down, pay attention to what you're doing right now.
3. **Choose a mindfulness technique.** Choose a technique appropriate for the moment. Examples include deep breathing, body scan, and mindful observation.
4. **Acknowledge distractions.** If you encounter any distractions, gently bring your focus back to your chosen technique, and continue.
5. **Reflect on your mindfulness.** Recognizing your progress and areas for growth helps you refine and deepen your mindfulness skills over time.[68]

By incorporating mindfulness into your daily routine, you'll discover its potential to sharpen your focus, improve emotional regulation, and support overall well-being.

Training Missions to Develop Mindfulness

Engage in activities such as these to enhance this superpower.

- **Mindful walking.** Consciously notice sensations and surroundings during walks.
- **The 5-4-3-2-1 Technique.** Name 5 things you can see, 4 things you can touch, 3 things you can hear, 2 things you can smell, and 1 thing you can taste.[69]

- **Mindful eating.** Take the time to slow down and enjoy your meals. Use all your senses to appreciate the aromas, colors, and textures.
- **Mindful movement.** Pay attention to your movements and how parts of your body flow as you move. Feel the energy in your body as you move, stretch, balance, and breathe.[70]

In the 2016 film *Batman v Superman: Dawn of Justice*, Batman demonstrates a remarkable level of mindfulness during his training and combat scenes, particularly through his sharp focus and heightened awareness of his surroundings. His battle with Superman, for instance, demands intense concentration as he carefully anticipates each move and meticulously plans his actions amidst the chaos of the fight. Batman's mindfulness is evident in his ability to stay fully present, maintain calm under immense pressure, and engage deeply in every situation, whether strategizing or in the thick of combat.[71]

Action Items

- Before you read further, take a few minutes to review the information presented in this section.
- Imagine yourself decades in the future (after many years of cultivating self-reflection and mindfulness) and how you use these superpowers to achieve your goals.
- Note how you currently address self-reflection and mindfulness in your daily life. Take pride in the progress you've already achieved in developing these superpowers.
- Evaluate the effectiveness of your current self-reflection and mindfulness practices in maintaining your wellness.

- If you decide that one or more of your current self-reflection and mindfulness practices must be improved, consider at least one for improvement.
- Develop a plan for implementing that improvement.

In wrapping up this chapter on holistic well-being, let's revisit our caped crusader, Batman. As the guardian of Gotham, he embodies the essence of balance, showcasing not only his prowess in battling adversaries but also his commitment to self-care and mental fortitude. Through his rigorous training regimen, meditative practices, and strategic reflections, Batman exemplifies how integrating stress management, wellness, self-reflection, and mindfulness into our daily lives empowers us to tackle challenges with resilience and grace. Just as Batman emerges from the shadows night after night, stronger and more determined, you can harness these holistic well-being superpowers to navigate life's complexities with ambition and purpose. Let the Dark Knight's dedication inspire you to cultivate a balanced, fulfilling life where your own well-being is the foundation of your personal success story.

In the next chapter, we'll explore how embracing personal responsibility, strategic thinking, resilience, and creativity can further empower you to become a real-life superhero.

CORE PERSONAL DEVELOPMENT

ersonal development means building your skills, knowledge, and mindset to create a strong foundation for your future. For teenagers, this isn't just about reaching immediate goals—it's about preparing for long-term growth and fulfillment. Think of Spider-Man, a young superhero balancing school life and extraordinary abilities. His story highlights how taking responsibility, viewing life strategically, overcoming setbacks, and thinking creatively are essential traits for heroes and anyone looking to grow and thrive.[1]

In the following pages, we'll explore the superpowers of personal responsibility, strategic thinking, resilience, and creativity. Join me now for a closer look at personal responsibility.

SUPERPOWER #5: PERSONAL RESPONSIBILITY

Personal responsibility is the ability to take ownership of your actions, your decisions, and their consequences. It involves being accountable for your choices and behaviors, understanding that your actions have an impact on yourself and others. This superpower requires self-discipline, honesty, and a willingness to admit mistakes and learn from them. Personal responsibility also includes fulfilling commitments, meeting obligations, and making decisions that align with your values. It is about recognizing that you have control over your life and making intentional choices that reflect that understanding.[2]

The Powers of Personal Responsibility

Like Peter Parker balancing his life as a high school student with his responsibilities as Spider-Man, when you understand that your actions, decisions, and attitudes directly influence your outcomes, you begin to live more intentionally and purposefully. This empowers you to take charge of your own path.

Building trust and respect is another key benefit of personal responsibility. When you consistently demonstrate dependability and accountability, people are more likely to trust you. This reputation can lead to valuable opportunities, such as leadership roles and internships.

Personal responsibility also enhances your problem-solving skills. By acknowledging your role in both creating and resolving issues, you shift from focusing on blame to finding constructive solutions. This proactive approach allows you to tackle problems with confidence and effectiveness.

As you take responsibility for your actions, finances, and personal growth, you cultivate independence and self-sufficiency. This enables you to make informed decisions and pursue your ambitions with clarity and determination.

Living with personal responsibility also aligns with integrity. It means standing by your commitments and doing the right thing even when no one is watching. This builds a legacy of trustworthiness and moral character.

Finally, embracing personal responsibility unlocks your potential. By committing to continual learning and self-improvement, you challenge yourself to grow and reach for your dreams. Mastering this superpower paves the way for a life of purpose, integrity, and success.[3]

How to Wield This Superpower

Here's a step-by-step process for mastering personal responsibility.

- **Acknowledge your role.** Recognize that you're the architect of your life. Accepting control over your actions and reactions empowers you to create positive change.
- **Set clear goals.** Define what you want to achieve. Writing down your goals reminds you of your targets.
- **Develop a plan.** Create a detailed plan to achieve your goals. Break down each goal into smaller, manageable tasks.
- **Take action.** Commit to your plan and follow through with your tasks. Stay disciplined and motivated.
- **Reflect and adjust as you go.** Regularly evaluate your progress. Adjust your plan as needed to overcome obstacles or optimize your approach.
- **Own your outcomes.** Celebrate your achievements and learn from your mistakes. Taking responsibility for your successes and failures builds resilience.

- **Seek support when needed.** Ask for advice and guidance from friends, family, or mentors.

By embracing these steps, you can master personal responsibility, empowering yourself to achieve your goals and create a positive, resilient, and accountable life.

Training Missions to Develop This Superpower

Engage in activities such as these to enhance your personal responsibility.

- **Prioritize your commitments.** To stay organized and responsible, create a schedule that includes schoolwork, chores, extracurricular activities, and hobbies.
- **Communicate effectively.** Express your thoughts and feelings respectfully and honestly to handle conflicts and resolve issues responsibly.
- **Practice self-discipline.** Once you set goals and establish a plan, avoid procrastination and follow through on your commitments.
- **Show respect and empathy.** Treat others with kindness, respect, and compassion. Understand the impact of your actions on others.
- **Take care of your health.** Eat a balanced diet, exercise regularly, and prioritize sufficient sleep to take responsibility for your health.
- **Manage finances responsibly.** Learn to budget and save if you earn money or receive an allowance. Spend money wisely.
- **Be honest and have integrity.** Be truthful in all your actions. Uphold your values and build trust and credibility with others.

- **Protect your online identity.** Be wise about what you share and who you share information with.
- **Take ownership of your education.** Attend classes regularly, complete assignments on time, and actively participate in your learning.[4]

In the 2002 film *Spider-Man*, after gaining his powers, Peter Parker initially uses them for personal gain, seeking fame and fortune. However, the tragic death of his Uncle Ben becomes a turning point in his life. Uncle Ben's iconic advice, "With great power comes great responsibility," resonates deeply with Peter when he realizes that his inaction allowed the criminal who killed his uncle to escape. Overcome with guilt, Peter fully accepts responsibility for his choices and commits himself to using his powers to protect others as Spider-Man. This pivotal moment highlights Peter's profound sense of personal responsibility, as he understands that his abilities are not meant for self-serving purposes, but for the greater good.[5]

Action Items

- Before you read further, take a few minutes to review the information presented in this section.
- Imagine yourself decades in the future (after many years of practicing personal responsibility) and how you use this superpower to achieve your goals.
- Note how you're currently addressing this superpower in your daily life. Take pride in the progress you've already achieved in developing personal responsibility.
- Evaluate the effectiveness of your current practices in cultivating this superpower. Think about how Spider-Man uses his sense of responsibility to shape his decisions and actions. How can you apply this same level of commitment

to your own life?

- If you decide that one or more of your current personal-responsibility practices need to be improved, consider at least one improvement.
- Develop a plan for implementing that improvement.

Now that we've addressed the strategic life skill of personal responsibility, let's move on to strategic thinking.

SUPERPOWER #6: STRATEGIC THINKING

Imagine you're standing at the edge of a vast, unexplored landscape. This is your life, full of endless possibilities. To navigate this terrain, you need more than just a map—you need a clear vision of where you want to go, the ambition to pursue your goals relentlessly, and the planning to make it all happen.

- *Vision* is the ability to see beyond the present and imagine a future filled with possibilities. It's about setting your sights on what you truly want to achieve and creating a guiding star that keeps you focused, motivated, and inspired. Your vision provides direction and purpose, helping you navigate through life's uncertainties with confidence.
- *Ambition* is the fuel that powers your journey. It's that inner drive that pushes you to strive for greatness, reach higher, and push past obstacles. Ambition is about being determined to turn big dreams into reality, relentlessly pursuing your goals, no matter how challenging they may seem.
- *Planning* is the bridge that connects your vision and ambition. It's the ability to make informed decisions, set priorities, manage resources, and anticipate potential

challenges. Planning involves more than organizing tasks —it's about making smart choices that pave the way for success and staying proactive to handle obstacles before they become roadblocks.

Spider-Man is a great example of a strategic thinker because, despite his raw talent and powers, he relies on his mind to solve problems and anticipate outcomes. Like Spider-Man, you can't depend on strength alone when facing tough challenges—you need strategy. His vision is to protect his city and loved ones, even if it puts him at risk. He sets clear priorities—stopping threats, saving civilians, and keeping his identity hidden. His ambition drives him to keep pushing forward, no matter how overwhelming the odds.

The Powers of Strategic Thinking

Strategic thinking transforms the way you approach your goals and aspirations. It allows you to look beyond immediate challenges and focus on the bigger picture. With a strong vision, you'll gain a clear sense of direction that helps you stay focused on what truly matters, even when life gets complicated. This clarity gives you a purpose and an anchor, so distractions or setbacks won't easily sway you.

Your ambition keeps the fire burning, pushing you to dream big and strive for greatness. Paired with a powerful vision, ambition becomes a relentless force, propelling you forward and keeping you motivated through both the highs and lows. It helps you stay resilient in the face of failure, fueling your belief that you can overcome any obstacle and continue moving toward your dreams.

Vision and ambition alone are not enough—planning turns your dreams into reality. It involves breaking down your goals into actionable steps, anticipating potential obstacles, and developing solutions before problems arise. When you plan strategically, you're not just hoping things will work out—you're actively shaping your path and setting yourself up for success. This skill builds confidence because you know you can handle whatever comes your way.

Mastering strategic thinking means being prepared to navigate life's complexities with purpose, drive, and a clear roadmap for success. It enables you to seize opportunities, adapt when circumstances change, and keep moving forward, even when the path ahead seems uncertain. Strategic thinking turns your potential into progress and your dreams into tangible achievements.

Creating a Vision Statement

Before you establish an objective and form a plan to achieve it, you first need to envision what you want to accomplish. That's the role of a vision statement. To make a personal vision statement, follow these steps.[6]

1. **Self-reflection.** Reflect on your passions, values, and aspirations.
2. **Write it down.** Keep it concise, no more than one sentence.
3. **Make it understandable.** Use language that resonates with you.
4. **Memorize and recite.** Reinforce your vision by repeating it often.
5. **Make it unique.** Ensure it truly represents you.
6. **Frame your priorities.** Guide your decision-making process.

Here are some examples of a vision statement for ambitious teens.

- **Aspiring scientist.** "I envision a future where I contribute to groundbreaking scientific discoveries that improve human health and the environment."
- **Budding entrepreneur.** "My vision is to create innovative businesses that solve everyday problems and inspire others to think creatively."
- **Future educator.** "I aim to empower and educate the next generation by fostering a love for learning and encouraging critical thinking."
- **Creative artist.** "I see myself expressing my creativity through art, inspiring others to find their voice and share their unique perspectives."
- **Tech innovator.** "My vision is to develop cutting-edge technologies that improve people's lives and help connect the world."
- **Healthcare professional.** "I envision a career dedicated to providing compassionate care and advancing medical knowledge to improve patient outcomes."
- **Community leader.** "I aspire to lead and uplift my community by promoting positive change."

Once you have your vision statement, you can establish goals for achieving your vision.

Goals: Charting Your Path to Success

Think of goals as a compass—guiding you through life's journeys, fueling your motivation, and giving meaning to your actions. By setting clear goals, you're not just creating targets to aim for—you're crafting a strategic map that shapes your decisions and actions, directing them toward achieving your dreams.

Start by identifying what truly excites you—your passions, interests, and strengths. Reflect on what matters most and what you hope to accomplish long term. Once you have a clear vision, segment your larger goals into smaller, manageable steps. Develop a detailed action plan that outlines how you'll approach each step along the way. Regularly review and reassess your goals to ensure they align with your evolving priorities and circumstances. Remember, it's normal for your objectives to change as you grow, so be flexible and willing to adjust your plans to keep them relevant and motivating.

One of the most effective ways to set goals is by using the SMART framework,[7] which ensures your goals are (1) specific, (2) measurable, (3) attainable, (4) relevant, and (5) time-bound. Being *specific* means defining your goals clearly—avoiding vague language and articulating exactly what you want to achieve. Making them *measurable* involves setting criteria for tracking your progress and recognizing when you're advancing. Goals should also be *attainable* —challenging yet within reach given your current resources. *Relevance* ensures that each goal fits your values and long-term vision. Finally, adding a *time frame* establishes a sense of urgency and provides a timeline to monitor your milestones.[8]

Using SMART goals transforms the goal-setting process into a structured, actionable plan, making it easier to stay focused and motivated. With this approach, your goals become more than just aspirations—they become a concrete blueprint guiding you toward personal fulfillment and success.

Let's apply these steps to an example goal: "Improve your math grades."

- **Be specific.** Refine the goal to make it specific. For example, "Raise my math grade from a C to a B."

- **Make it measurable.** Determine how you will measure progress. For example, "Achieve an average 80% or higher score on math tests and assignments."
- **Ensure it is attainable.** Assess whether the goal is realistic. Consider factors like your study habits, available resources, and support. For example, "With consistent studying and seeking help from my teacher or tutor, improving my math grade is attainable."
- **Be relevant.** Reflect on why this goal is important. For example, "Improving my math grade is important because I want to excel in all subjects and have more opportunities in the future."
- **Set a timeframe.** Set a deadline for achieving the goal. For example, "Raise my math grade to a B by the end of this quarter."

How to Wield This Superpower

Spider-Man's planning is one of his most important powers. He constantly analyzes the environment, considers his opponent's strengths and weaknesses, and uses creative tactics to outsmart foes. He adapts quickly, using his web-shooters, agility, and surroundings to his advantage. Even in the heat of battle, he thinks several steps ahead, anticipates attacks, and sets traps. He's a master of turning weaknesses into strengths and making snap decisions that align with his long-term goal of safeguarding his community.

Mastering strategic thinking can be guided by the 6 Ps, a framework commonly used in business to ensure alignment and collaboration toward a common goal.[9] This approach can also be easily adapted to personal life.

1. **Purpose.** Start by defining your vision and ensuring it aligns with your core values and beliefs. Creating or updating a vision statement can help.

2. **Perspective.** Step outside of your own viewpoint and consider the situation from multiple perspectives. Evaluate your strengths and weaknesses, identify potential opportunities, and assess any risks or threats that could hinder your progress. Consider the information and resources you might need to succeed.

3. **Plan.** Explore alternative strategies and solutions and then determine the specific actions required to achieve your goal. Establish SMART goals—specific, measurable, achievable, relevant, and time-bound—to guide your efforts.[10]

4. **Prioritize.** Identify the actions that need to be taken first to achieve your objective. Sometimes, it may be necessary to mitigate risks (such as by enhancing your skills or knowledge) before moving forward with other steps. Map out a timeline to guide your progress.

5. **Pace.** Once you have a timeline, establish a pace for each activity. Recognize that some tasks may require more time and effort than others, and adjust your pace accordingly to stay on track.

6. **Performance.** Regularly measure and monitor your performance to ensure you're making progress toward your goal. This ongoing feedback allows you to make adjustments and improvements as needed. Reflect on your achievements and celebrate your victories to maintain motivation.

By following this process and using the 6 Ps, you can turn your vision into actionable goals and create a clear, adaptable path to success.[11]

Training Missions to Develop This Superpower

Engage in the following training missions to cultivate the super-power of strategic thinking, which includes vision, ambition, and planning.

- **Play strategy games.** Games like Monopoly, chess, UNO, or strategy-based video games help you practice thinking ahead, planning for various scenarios, evaluating risks, and adapting to changing circumstances—all critical components of strategic thinking.
- **Challenge yourself with logic puzzles and riddles.** Completing patterns, solving Sudoku, and answering riddles are excellent for sharpening your problem-solving abilities and boosting short-term memory. Such activities can help both hemispheres of your brain work in harmony.
- **Look for connections in everyday life.** Practice identifying hidden patterns and connections in your environment. Noticing these links will help you develop a mindset that sees opportunities others may overlook.
- **Discuss your ideas with others.** Talk about your plans and strategies with people you trust. This practice can provide valuable feedback, reveal potential blind spots, and expose you to new perspectives that will enhance your strategic approach.
- **Never stop learning.** Continuously seek new information and explore learning opportunities to expand your knowledge. A broader understanding of various subjects will deepen your insight and enable you to make more informed decisions.

- **Take time to reflect and think twice.** Instead of making impulsive decisions, pause and carefully consider your options, weigh the potential outcomes, and think through the possible consequences of your actions.
- **Have a plan B.** Being prepared for unexpected obstacles by creating a backup plan doesn't mean plan A will fail—it simply equips you to handle setbacks with confidence and resilience.
- **Have faith in your abilities.** The answers may not be apparent right away, but trust that with patience and persistence, you'll find the right solution.

In the 2017 film *Spider-Man: Homecoming*, Peter Parker faces a formidable adversary, the Vulture, whose advanced technology far surpasses Peter's resources. Stripped of Tony Stark's high-tech suit, Peter must rely on his strategic thinking to dismantle the Vulture's illegal weapons operations. He carefully tracks the shipment routes, gathering intelligence and planning a way to stop the Vulture without relying on sophisticated gadgets. In the final battle, Peter strategically targets the Vulture's wings, understanding that disabling them will neutralize his enemy. This showcases Peter's ability to think ahead and remain composed under pressure, relying on his intellect and resourcefulness to overcome challenges.[12]

Action Items

- Before you read further, take a few minutes to consider the information presented in this section.
- Imagine yourself decades in the future (after many years of cultivating strategic thinking) and how you use this superpower to achieve your goals.

- Note how you currently employ strategic thinking in your daily life. Take pride in the progress you've already achieved in developing this superpower.
- Evaluate the effectiveness of your current practices to cultivate strategic thinking.
- If you decide that your current efforts to cultivate this superpower need to be improved, consider at least one improvement to be made in the coming weeks, months, or year.
- Develop a plan for implementing that improvement.

Now that we've addressed the superpower of strategic thinking, let's move on to resilience.

SUPERPOWER #7: RESILIENCE

Resilience is the ability to withstand and recover from adversity, challenges, or setbacks. It involves maintaining a steady mindset in the face of difficulties and adapting to changing circumstances without losing focus or motivation. This superpower enables you to navigate hardships with persistence and determination, allowing you to bounce back from failures or disappointments. Resilience is about staying mentally strong, maintaining emotional balance, and continuing to move forward despite obstacles. It requires flexibility, perseverance, and the ability to learn from tough experiences, ultimately allowing you to grow stronger and more capable in the process.[13]

The Powers of Resilience

Mastering resilience can transform your life. It equips you to tackle problems with a constructive mindset, helping you break challenges into smaller steps and persist until you find a solution. This strength empowers you to stay grounded, manage stress, and maintain emotional stability, even when faced with difficult situations. The ability to handle adversity with composure builds your confidence, reinforcing your belief in your own capabilities.

Resilience also strengthens your relationships by enabling you to form healthier, more supportive connections. When you navigate setbacks effectively, you become a source of stability and positivity for others, which deepens your bonds and creates more meaningful interactions.

Resilient individuals are adaptable, capable of thriving in unfamiliar circumstances and adjusting to change with ease—an essential skill in today's ever-evolving world. This adaptability, combined with perseverance, keeps you focused on your long-term goals, helps you learn from setbacks, and drives continuous growth.

Physically, resilience allows you to manage stress more effectively, reducing the impact of anxiety and contributing to better health. It empowers you to take control of your life, face uncertainties with strength, and respond to challenges proactively. Developing resilience sets the foundation for lasting success, stronger relationships, and a more empowered life.[14]

How to Wield This Superpower

Here's a step-by-step process for mastering resilience.

1. **Acknowledge your feelings.** Recognize and accept your emotions. Give yourself space to process them, allowing you to move forward with clarity.
2. **Analyze the situation.** Objectively assess setbacks, understanding what went wrong and identifying areas for improvement.
3. **Reframe your mindset.** View challenges as growth opportunities. Ask yourself what lessons you can learn from the experience.
4. **Review and revise.** Revisit your goals, strategies, and action steps. If necessary, make adjustments to stay on track.
5. **Develop a support system.** Surround yourself with positive influences who encourage and uplift you.[15]
6. **Practice self-care.** Prioritize your physical, emotional, and mental well-being through healthy eating, regular exercise, and rest.
7. **Stay persistent.** Keep moving forward, knowing setbacks are temporary and persistence is key to overcoming obstacles.
8. **Celebrate your strengths.** Acknowledge your resilience and progress, using past successes as reminders of your ability to thrive.

By following these steps, you can build resilience and face life's challenges with greater confidence and strength.

Training Missions to Develop This Superpower

Engage in activities such as these to help enhance your resilience.

- **Volunteering.** Volunteer work teaches empathy and perspective, reinforcing emotional resilience through diverse experiences.
- **Team sports or group activities.** Joining sports teams or group activities helps you cope with wins and losses, handle criticism, and work cooperatively, building emotional endurance and interpersonal skills.
- **New skills.** Overcoming obstacles in learning new skills builds confidence and proves that persistence pays off.
- **Mindfulness.** Regular mindfulness practices enhance mental resilience, helping manage stress and improve focus.
- **Reflective practices.** Keeping a journal or reflecting on daily experiences helps you process experiences deeply, learn from mistakes, and appreciate growth.
- **Resilient role models.** Learning about others who have overcome adversity can inspire and offer practical strategies for handling your own challenges.

In the 2019 film *Spider-Man: Far From Home*, Peter Parker feels overwhelmed and defeated after Mysterio manipulates him and reveals his true identity to the world. Despite his initial doubts, Peter bounces back, showing resilience by taking on Mysterio again. He learns from his previous failures, adapts his tactics, and ultimately defeats Mysterio in their second battle, reclaiming his role as Spider-Man. Peter's ability to overcome emotional and physical setbacks, rebuild his confidence, and persevere against a powerful enemy showcases his resilience.[16]

Action Items

- Before you read further, take a few minutes to consider the information presented in this section.
- Imagine yourself decades in the future (after many years of cultivating resilience) and how you use this superpower to achieve your goals.
- Note how you currently practice resilience in your daily life. Take pride in the progress you've already achieved in developing this superpower.
- Evaluate the effectiveness of your current efforts to cultivate resilience.
- If you decide your efforts to cultivate this superpower need to be improved, consider at least one improvement you can make over the coming weeks, months, or year.
- Develop a plan for implementing that improvement.

Now that we've addressed the strategic life skill of resilience, let's move on to creativity.

SUPERPOWER #8: CREATIVITY

Creativity is the ability to generate new ideas, think outside traditional parameters, and approach situations from fresh perspectives. It involves using imagination and originality to solve problems, express ideas, or create something innovative. This superpower allows you to explore different possibilities, make connections between seemingly unrelated concepts, and develop unique solutions. Creativity is not limited to artistic expression—it can be applied to various areas of life, from science and technology to everyday decision-making. It requires curiosity, openness, and a willingness to experiment with new approaches and ideas.[17]

The Powers of Creativity

Spider-Man's quick thinking and ability to come up with innovative solutions—whether using his web-slinging skills to stop a villain or creating new technology for his suit—illustrate the power of creativity to sharpen your problem-solving skills, enabling you to approach challenges from different angles and develop innovative solutions. Creativity also fosters adaptability, helping you become more flexible and open to new ideas, which makes it easier to adjust to changing circumstances.

Creativity can bring remarkable benefits to your personal and professional life. Engaging in creative activities boosts your confidence, as it encourages you to take risks and trust in your abilities. It also improves communication skills, allowing you to express complex ideas more effectively and connect with others on a deeper level. Creativity offers an emotional outlet, promoting emotional well-being by reducing stress and fostering mental health.[18]

Sharing your creative work strengthens personal connections, as it fosters empathy and understanding between you and others. Creativity also increases your productivity and focus, helping you enter a highly concentrated state that enhances your performance. Additionally, it encourages lifelong learning and growth by sparking curiosity and pushing the boundaries of what you can achieve.

Through creative endeavors, you express your unique identity, helping you stand out and develop a strong sense of self. Embracing creativity as a strategic skill empowers you to navigate life's challenges with originality and resilience, leading to a more vibrant, purposeful, and fulfilling life.

How to Wield This Superpower

Here's a step-by-step process for mastering creativity.

1. **Embrace curiosity.** Ask questions about everything you encounter to spark creative thinking.
2. **Start an idea journal.** Capture every idea that pops into your head without judgment.[19]
3. **Create a stimulating environment.** Surround yourself with stimuli that inspire you.
4. **Engage in play.** Engage in playful activities to relax and encourage unexpected insights.[20]
5. **Practice divergent thinking.** Brainstorm multiple solutions to problems, no matter how outlandish.
6. **Expect failure.** Understand that failure is part of the creative process and learn from it.
7. **Set aside time for creativity.** Dedicate specific time for creative activities to strengthen your creative muscles.
8. **Reflect and adjust.** Periodically review and improve your ideas.
9. **Stay inspired.** Seek new sources of inspiration through workshops, books, and creative communities.

By consistently nurturing these habits, you'll unlock your full creative potential and wield creativity as a powerful tool to tackle challenges and achieve your goals.

Training Missions to Develop This Superpower

Engaging in activities such as these can enhance your creativity.[21]

- **Drawing and doodling.** Keep a sketchbook for visualizing ideas and sparking new insights.

- **Reading widely.** Read across various genres to broaden your mind and fuel your imagination.
- **Writing stories or poetry.** Use creative writing to express thoughts and explore new ideas.
- **Engaging in DIY projects.** Try crafting or upcycling to exercise problem-solving and innovative thinking.
- **Participating in drama or dance.** Join performing arts to develop creativity, confidence, and teamwork skills.
- **Attending workshops and classes.** Enroll in creative workshops to learn new techniques and inspire your skills.
- **Engaging in mindfulness.** Practice mindfulness to clear your mind and open it to creative thoughts.
- **Traveling and exploring new places.** Visit new places to expose yourself to different cultures and experiences.
- **Collaborating with others.** Work on projects with others to share ideas and learn from different perspectives.

In the 2021 film *Spider-Man: No Way Home*, during the final battle against multiple villains from alternate universes, Peter Parker teams up with other versions of Spider-Man from different realities to creatively devise a solution. Instead of merely fighting the villains, Peter and his counterparts use their combined scientific knowledge and creativity to engineer antidotes that cure each villain, restoring them to their original forms. This innovative problem-solving approach allows Peter to resolve the conflict without resorting to unnecessary violence. Peter demonstrates his creativity and resourcefulness by choosing science over brute force, showcasing his ability to think outside established patterns in high-stakes situations.[22]

Action Items

- Before you read further, take a few minutes to consider the information presented in this section.
- Imagine yourself decades in the future (after many years of cultivating creativity) and how you use this superpower to achieve your goals.
- Note how you currently practice creativity in your daily life. Take pride in the progress you've already achieved in developing this superpower.
- Evaluate the effectiveness of your current practices to cultivate creativity. Think about how Spider-Man uses his creativity to shape his decisions and actions. How can you apply this superpower in your own life?
- If you decide that your current efforts to cultivate creativity need to be improved, consider at least one improvement.
- Develop a plan for implementing that improvement.

In this chapter, we've explored the foundational skills of personal development, emphasizing the importance of personal responsibility, strategic thinking, resilience, and creativity. These core aspects provide the groundwork for personal growth and success in various areas of life.

Let's circle back to Spider-Man, an emblematic figure whose story arcs within the pages of comic books illuminate a journey of self-development. Under the mask of Spider-Man, Peter Parker shows great commitment to personal responsibility, strategic thinking, resilience in the face of adversity, and an innovative spirit. As you venture beyond this chapter, let Spider-Man inspire you to embrace your new superpowers on the path to becoming the hero of your own story.

Now that you've learned how to build a strong foundation in core personal development, it's time to take your skills to the next level for navigating the complexities of the modern world. In the upcoming chapter, we'll address analytical skills, critical thinking, problem-solving, and decision-making—competencies you'll need to sharpen your cognitive abilities and unlock your full potential.

ANALYTICAL AND DECISION-MAKING SKILLS

I n a world of opportunities and challenges, navigating complex situations with grace and foresight empowers you to excel in any endeavor you pursue. Here, we delve into the competencies that distinguish the good from the great—analytical skills, critical thinking, problem-solving, and decision-making skills.

An example of a superhero who demonstrates these skills is Iron Man,[1] whose strength lies in his suit and extraordinary ability to analyze complex situations, and make critical decisions under pressure. His journey from a brilliant inventor to a heroic figure exemplifies how analytical and decision-making skills can create remarkable inventions and lives.[2]

As we explore these strategic life skills, keep in mind that each is interlinked, forming a synergistic framework that will propel you toward your ambitions and equip you to thrive in an ever-changing world. We'll start with the superpower of analytical skills.

SUPERPOWER #9: ANALYTICAL SKILLS

Analytical skills are the ability to methodically break down information, data, or problems into smaller parts to better understand and interpret them. This superpower involves recognizing patterns, identifying trends, and making connections between different pieces of information. It requires logical thinking, attention to detail, and the ability to organize complex information in a clear and manageable way. Mastering analytical skills means applying structured approaches to evaluate data, draw conclusions, and make informed decisions based on thorough examination and reasoning.[3]

The Powers of Analytical Skills

Iron Man's analytical abilities allow him to quickly assess complex situations, like diagnosing a malfunction in his suit mid-battle or outsmarting a villain. Similarly, by honing your analytical abilities, you lay the groundwork for success in school, creative ventures, and your future career.

Achieving mastery of analytical skills can significantly enhance your life by sharpening your ability to approach challenges with clarity and precision. You'll be able to break down complex problems into smaller, manageable parts, making it easier to develop effective solutions.[4] When it comes to decision-making, you'll rely on logic and facts, which leads to more informed and successful choices in both personal and academic settings.

As you deepen your understanding of systems and patterns, your creativity will also expand, enabling you to develop innovative solutions to challenges. These skills directly contribute to better academic performance, helping you grasp complex subjects and excel in areas that require critical thinking. In the professional world, having strong analytical skills sets you apart—employers seek individuals who can interpret data, analyze situations, and make well-informed decisions, opening up more opportunities for career growth.[5]

How to Wield This Superpower

Here's a step-by-step process for mastering analytical skills.[6]

1. **Understanding the basics.** Learn to gather information, break down problems, and analyze data. Engage with puzzles, games, and activities that challenge your reasoning abilities.
2. **Developing a curious mindset.** Encourage yourself to question everything. Ask, "What is the evidence?" and "Why is this the case?" to delve deeper into issues.
3. **Practicing critical thinking.** Assess the quality of information, identify biases, and consider other viewpoints. Evaluate sources for credibility and weigh the evidence.
4. **Learning from experts.** Seek mentors, teachers, or professionals who excel in analytical thinking. Watch how they solve problems and make decisions. Read books, listen to podcasts, and explore articles on critical thinking and problem-solving.
5. **Applying skills in real-world scenarios.** Take on projects requiring analytical skills, such as planning events or starting a small business. These experiences will help you gather data, analyze it, and make informed decisions.
6. **Reflecting and refining.** Reflect on your experiences to refine your analytical process. Consider what worked well and what could be improved to sharpen your skills.

By following these steps, you can develop and enhance your analytical skills, enabling you to make informed decisions and solve complex problems effectively.

Training Missions to Develop This Superpower

Engage in activities such as these to enhance your analytical skills.[7]

- **Read mystery or suspense novels.** These types of books often spark questions like who did it and why.
- **Be more observant.** Paying attention to smaller details helps you to understand how things work.
- **Practice mind mapping.** Use mind mapping for complex topics or problems to analyze information and connections clearly.[8]
- **Take exercise classes that involve patterns.** Memorizing steps in activities like a dance class enhances cognitive abilities and improves the understanding of sequences and anticipating what comes next.
- **Join a debate club.** You'll see how others process information and generate their thoughts and ideas.
- **Learn to code.** Coding teaches logical thinking, step-by-step problem-solving, and an understanding of digital tools' mechanics.
- **Read the news.** Expose yourself to various subjects and practice critical reading by questioning authors' assumptions, arguments, and evidence.

In the 2008 film *Iron Man*, after being captured by terrorists and ordered to build weapons, Tony Stark uses his sharp analytical skills to assess the materials available to him. Rather than constructing the missile he's been tasked with, Tony ingeniously designs and builds the first prototype of the Iron Man suit using only scrap parts. By carefully analyzing the functionality of each component and structure, he creates a highly advanced piece of technology from minimal resources. This situation underscores Tony's ability to break down complex problems into manageable parts, demonstrating his keen analytical mind and capacity to develop innovative solutions, even under extreme pressure.[9]

Action Items

- Before you read further, take a few minutes to consider the information presented in this section.
- Imagine yourself decades in the future (after many years of cultivating analytical skills) and how you use this superpower to achieve your goals.
- Note how you currently practice analytical skills in your daily life. Take pride in the progress you've already achieved in developing this superpower.
- Evaluate the effectiveness of your current practices to cultivate analytical skills.
- If you decide that your current efforts to cultivate these skills need to be improved, consider at least one improvement.
- Develop a plan for implementing that improvement.

Now that we've addressed analytical skills, let's move on to critical thinking.

SUPERPOWERS #10 & 11: CRITICAL THINKING AND PROBLEM-SOLVING SKILLS

Critical thinking and problem-solving are distinct superpowers, yet they share many similarities. The best way to understand them is through comparison. Let's start by defining and explaining each.

- *Critical thinking* is the ability to analyze information objectively, evaluate different perspectives, and draw well-reasoned conclusions. It's about questioning assumptions, examining evidence, and considering various viewpoints before making a decision. When individuals engage in critical thinking, they ask "why" and "how" about the information they receive. They actively challenge assumptions, weigh the evidence, and differentiate between opinion and fact. Critical thinkers also recognize biases—both their own and those of others. It's a reflective and structured approach to thinking, often involving steps like identifying the issue, analyzing the context, and seeking clarity.[10]
- *Problem-solving skills* refer to the ability to identify solutions to specific challenges or obstacles. It involves diagnosing the issue, brainstorming potential solutions, evaluating those solutions, and implementing the best one. In problem-solving, individuals are focused on fixing a situation that requires a clear, actionable response. Unlike critical thinking, which may involve broader, more abstract reasoning, problem-solving is goal-oriented and practical. It often requires creativity, logical thinking, and collaboration. Problem-solving can be more immediate, as it involves coming up with strategies that work in real time.

Comparing Critical Thinking and Problem-Solving Skills

- **Focus.** Critical thinking emphasizes analyzing and evaluating information and ideas broadly, whereas problem-solving is more action-oriented, focusing on finding practical solutions to specific challenges.
- **Scope.** Critical thinking often deals with abstract, theoretical issues (e.g., evaluating arguments or evidence), while problem-solving is focused on concrete, real-world obstacles (e.g., logistical problems or interpersonal conflicts).
- **Process.** Both require analysis and evaluation, but critical thinking is more reflective, encouraging you to consider all sides of an issue, while problem-solving pushes you toward a solution, often through creative brainstorming and practical steps.
- **Benefits.** Critical thinking strengthens your ability to make sound judgments and learn, whereas problem-solving hones your ability to tackle challenges directly and efficiently.

Just as Iron Man questions assumptions and evaluates his options before making decisions in high-pressure situations, mastering critical thinking and problem-solving skills will empower you to approach issues logically and clearly.

How to Wield These Superpowers

In the real world, critical thinking helps you navigate complex ideas, while problem-solving equips you to tackle practical challenges. Throughout your life, however, you'll encounter a wide range of situations that fall anywhere between the theoretical and the practical. Many of these challenges will require a blend of both critical thinking and problem-solving to find the best resolution. Whether you're analyzing a complex issue or working through a hands-on problem, knowing how to apply these skills effectively will help you make informed, confident decisions.

Here's a process for mastering both critical thinking[11] and problem-solving.[12]

1. **Identify and define.** Start by understanding the issue. For critical thinking, ask yourself: What's the concern? Why does it matter? What could happen if it's ignored? For problem-solving, pinpoint what's going wrong and why it's important. Be sure to differentiate between surface symptoms and deeper root causes.

2. **Break it down.** When necessary, break the issue or problem into smaller, more manageable parts. This makes complex challenges feel less overwhelming and easier to approach step by step.

3. **Gather relevant information.** Collect information from a variety of reliable sources. The more perspectives you consider, the better prepared you'll be to find an informed solution.

4. **Analyze the information.** Look for patterns, connections, and assumptions.[13] Ask critical questions such as: What are the main points? Are there any gaps in the information?

5. **Evaluate the evidence.** Assess the credibility and relevance of the information you've gathered. Consider whether any sources have biases and weigh the evidence to determine how it applies to the issue.

6. **Consider alternatives.** Brainstorm a range of possible solutions without judgment. This opens the door to creative thinking. Once you have options, evaluate the pros and cons of each.

7. **Evaluate and select a solution.** Assess each potential solution based on feasibility, impact, and the resources required. Choose the best option, and it's always wise to have a backup plan.

By following these steps, you can approach a wide range of issues with confidence, clarity, and effectiveness.

Example: Applying Critical Thinking and Problem-Solving in Real Life

Imagine you're deciding which extracurricular activities to join at school.

1. **Identify and define.** Your goal is to choose activities that match your interests and strengths and align with your future aspirations.

2. **Break it down.** This step may not be necessary here, but if you're juggling multiple interests, consider categorizing activities by type, such as academic, athletic, or creative.

3. **Gather relevant information.** Research the clubs and teams available. Talk to current members, attend introductory meetings, and read any information or reviews available to help you understand what each activity involves.

4. **Analyze the information.** Compare your options by considering factors like time commitment, potential for skill development, opportunities for leadership, and how much you think you'd enjoy the activity.

5. **Evaluate the evidence.** Weigh feedback from peers, teachers, and mentors, and reflect on how each activity aligns with your personal interests and goals.
6. **Consider alternatives.** Explore all the activities available, even those you may not have initially considered. You might discover a new passion or interest.
7. **Evaluate and select a solution.** Choose the activity that best suits your interests, schedule, and goals. Be open to adjusting your choice if your priorities or interests change.

By using this approach, you can make an informed and thoughtful decision about which extracurriculars will benefit you the most.

Training Missions to Develop Critical Thinking

Engage in these activities to strengthen your critical-thinking skills.

- **Reflective writing.** Regularly write about your experiences, beliefs, and decisions to examine how you think. This practice helps you spot patterns and evaluate the thought processes behind your actions.
- **Analyze media critically.** Consume news and media from multiple sources. Practice identifying biases, assumptions, and the motives behind each source's presentation of information.[14]
- **Listen to understand.** When talking to others, listen without forming your response immediately. Focus entirely on what they have to say before offering your perspective. This builds a deeper understanding.

- **Solve real-world issues.** Apply critical thinking to address challenges in your nation, community, or family. These real-world experiences will help you sharpen your analytical skills.
- **Use the "5 Whys" Technique.** When facing an issue, ask "Why?" five times. Each time you get an answer, ask why again. By the fifth why, you'll often discover the root cause of the problem.[15]
- **Play devil's advocate.** Take on the opposite side of your own opinion to see things from a different perspective. This will challenge your views and help you discover new insights.[16]

In the 2010 film *Iron Man 2*, Tony Stark is confronted with the life-threatening toxicity of his arc reactor, realizing that the palladium core is slowly poisoning him. Demonstrating his critical thinking skills, Tony revisits his father's research and uncovers clues that point to the creation of a new, sustainable element. By synthesizing this element, Tony successfully solves the reactor issue and saves his life. His ability to question assumptions, delve into the scientific details, and apply his knowledge exemplifies his critical thinking, enabling him to develop a groundbreaking solution in a life-or-death situation.[17]

Training Missions to Develop Problem-Solving Skills

Engage in these activities to develop your problem-solving skills.

- **Embrace a growth mindset.** Believe in your ability to learn and improve. View every problem as an opportunity to grow rather than as a roadblock.

- **Practice creative thinking.** Break out of conventional thinking patterns through brainstorming, mind mapping, or solving lateral thinking puzzles.[18] These techniques push you to think outside conventional patterns.
- **Learn from others.** Observe how mentors, historical figures, or even characters from books and movies solve problems. Analyze their strategies and consider how you can apply similar approaches.
- **Build technical skills.** Identify areas where you need to improve and take action. Whether through courses, books, or practice, mastering new skills equips you to tackle more complex problems.
- **Seek diverse challenges.** Step outside your comfort zone by exploring new subjects, taking on different projects, or engaging in unfamiliar activities. Exposure to varied challenges enhances your adaptability.

In the 2013 film *Iron Man 3*, Tony Stark is left stranded without access to his usual advanced technology after the Mandarin forces destroy his home. Forced to rely on basic tools, Tony demonstrates his ingenuity by crafting makeshift gadgets to infiltrate the enemy's hideout and continue his mission. His quick thinking and ability to adapt under pressure highlight his remarkable resourcefulness. This situation exemplifies Tony's problem-solving skills, as he devises creative solutions in the face of adversity, using innovation and sharp instincts to overcome unexpected challenges.[19]

Action Items

- Before you read further, take a few minutes to consider the information presented in this section.

- Imagine yourself decades in the future (after many years of cultivating critical thinking and problem-solving skills), and how you use these superpowers to achieve your goals.
- Note how you currently employ critical thinking and problem-solving skills in your daily life. Take pride in the progress you've already achieved in developing these superpowers.
- Evaluate the effectiveness of your current practices to cultivate critical thinking and problem-solving skills.
- If you decide that your current efforts to cultivate these superpowers need improvement, consider at least one improvement in the coming weeks, months, or year.
- Develop a plan for implementing that improvement.

Now that we've addressed the superpowers of critical thinking and problem-solving skills, let's move on to decision-making skills.

SUPERPOWER #12: DECISION-MAKING SKILLS

Decision-making skills are the ability to evaluate different options, assess potential outcomes, and choose the most effective course of action. This superpower involves a process of gathering information, analyzing facts, and considering various perspectives before reaching a conclusion. It requires thinking critically, weighing pros and cons, and making choices with clarity and confidence, even when faced with uncertainty or pressure. Mastering decision-making skills means developing a systematic approach to making thoughtful, informed decisions in various situations, from daily life choices to more complex and challenging situations.[20]

The Powers of Decision-Making Skills

Iron Man's ability to weigh risks and make fast, informed decisions—whether it's choosing how to battle an enemy or developing a new suit upgrade—demonstrates how vital strong decision-making skills are for success.

As you grow more decisive, you'll naturally develop stronger leadership qualities. Good leaders make sound, timely decisions, and this ability will position you to inspire and guide others. Additionally, by reducing the uncertainty that often leads to stress, decision-making offers peace of mind, allowing you to move forward with less anxiety and greater focus.

The Nexus Between Superpowers

You've likely noticed that all the superpowers discussed in this chapter equip you to make better decisions. Skills like analytical thinking, critical thinking, and problem-solving offer valuable insights that guide your choices. In the previous chapter, we explored how strategic thinking forms the foundation for making strategic decisions. More broadly, every superpower in this book —from ambition to wellness management—relies on the ability to make informed decisions. In each instance, information must be carefully assessed before reaching a conclusion.

It's fitting to view decision-making as the nexus, or the common thread, connecting all the superpowers. At the core of wielding any superpower is the ability to gather and assess information before deciding on a course of action. While each life skill plays a role in personal development, decision-making is the most crucial. Ultimately, our lives can be seen as the sum of our decisions. Mastering the superpower of decision-making empowers us to navigate life's challenges with precision and care.

Ethical Decisions

Ethical decision-making involves making choices that align with moral principles and contribute positively to the well-being of others and society. Recognize when choices have moral implications. Ethical values affecting decision-making include trustworthiness, respect, responsibility, fairness, caring, and citizenship. Evaluate how decisions affect you, others, your community, and your nation. By consistently practicing ethical decision-making, you build a foundation of integrity and trust, guiding your actions to positively impact your life and those around you.[21]

Iron Man's internal conflict about the ethics of his technology shows how critical it is to evaluate not just what you *can* do, but what you *should* do. Ethical decision-making ensures that your actions reflect your values and contribute to a better world.

How to Wield This Superpower

To effectively wield the superpower of decision-making, you need a clear process that helps you assess your options, consider potential outcomes, and commit to a course of action. The decisions you make shape your path, and using this skill strategically will ensure you're moving toward your goals with confidence.

Here's a five-step process to master this superpower.

1. **Clarify the decision.** Every decision begins with clarity. Before you act, define the problem or choice at hand. Ask yourself: What decision needs to be made? Are there specific outcomes I am trying to achieve? By understanding the decision's scope, you can focus your energy on finding the best solution.

2. **Gather relevant information.** Once you've identified the decision, it's time to gather all the necessary information. Look at the facts, consult experts if needed, and assess past experiences that might inform this choice. This step prevents you from making decisions based on incomplete or incorrect assumptions. The more informed you are, the better positioned you'll be to choose wisely.

3. **Identify your options.** Now, consider all possible options. Don't just focus on the most obvious solution—think creatively. What alternatives are available? Are there risks with any of these choices? Weigh the pros and cons of each option, keeping in mind how each aligns with your long-term vision and values.

4. **Evaluate potential outcomes.** Every decision has consequences. Picture the outcomes for each option. How will each choice impact your life and your goals? What, if any, ethical implications are involved? This step involves using both analytical skills and critical thinking to forecast the effects of your decision. Consider the short- and long-term impacts and whether you're ready to handle them.

5. **Make the decision and take action.** After evaluating your options, it's time to decide. Trust the process you've followed, knowing you've weighed the facts, considered your goals, and evaluated possible outcomes. Once you've chosen, commit to it fully. Take action confidently but be prepared to adapt if new information arises.[22]

Remember, decision-making is a dynamic superpower. Every choice you make teaches you something, and by practicing this process, you'll improve your ability to navigate even the toughest decisions.

Training Missions to Develop This Superpower

Engage in activities such as these to enhance your decision-making skills.

- **Practice deliberate choices.** Start small by making deliberate choices in daily life. Weigh the pros and cons of each option.
- **Reflect on past decisions.** Consider what went well and what didn't. Document your thoughts and insights in a journal for future reference.
- **Embrace uncertainty and take calculated risks.** Understand that not all decisions will have clear outcomes. Learn to embrace uncertainty and take risks after evaluating potential outcomes.
- **Develop emotional intelligence.** Practice emotional intelligence by being aware of your emotions and how they influence your choices and those of others. Techniques like mindfulness and deep breathing can help.
- **Delay decision-making when you're feeling emotionally intense.** It's best to take a break, process your emotions, and return to the decision so you don't make the wrong choice based on strong feelings.
- **Allow a reasonable amount of time.** Rushing to make a decision can cause you to miss important information. On the other hand, if your research is not turning up new information, you might risk *analysis paralysis*, the fear of committing a mistake that stops you from making the decision.

In the 2019 film *Avengers: Endgame*, Tony Stark's decision to wield the Infinity Gauntlet and snap Thanos and his army out of existence exemplifies the gravity of his decision-making skills. Aware that using the Gauntlet will cost him his life, Tony chooses to act, fully understanding that it is the only way to save the universe. This moment underscores his ability to make high-stakes decisions while considering the immense consequences. Tony's choice reflects his capacity to weigh risks and benefits, ultimately sacrificing himself for the greater good and taking full responsibility for the outcome.[23]

Action Items

- Before you read further, take a few minutes to consider the information presented in this section.
- Imagine yourself decades in the future (after many years of cultivating decision-making skills) and how you use this superpower to achieve your goals.
- Note how you currently employ decision-making skills in your daily life. Take pride in the progress you've already achieved in developing this superpower.
- Evaluate the effectiveness of your current practices to cultivate decision-making skills.
- If you decide that your current efforts to cultivate this superpower need to be improved, consider at least one improvement you can make in the coming weeks, months, or year.
- Develop a plan for implementing that improvement.

As we close this chapter on analytical and decision-making skills, it's fitting to return to the inspiring example of Iron Man. His transformation from a gifted inventor to a globally recognized superhero underscores the impact that analytical and decision-making skills can have. Tony Stark's ability to confront challenges, both in his personal life and on the battlefield, with a calm, calculated approach is a testament to the power of these skills. Just as

Iron Man assembles his suit piece by piece, you can build your future with the same deliberate and thoughtful strategies.

Now that you're equipped with analytical and decision-making skills, we'll address communication and interpersonal skills in the next chapter.

4

COMMUNICATION AND
INTERPERSONAL SKILLS

C onsider Wonder Woman (Diana Prince), who exemplifies powerful communication and interpersonal skills through her diplomatic nature, empathy, and ability to unite people from different backgrounds. As an ambassador for peace, Wonder Woman consistently resolves conflicts through strength, negotiation, understanding, and compassion. Her leadership style is rooted in her ability to connect with people personally, inspiring trust and collaboration.

This chapter addresses the art and science of effectively interacting with others. It's your guide to reaching the pinnacle of personal achievement and cultivating meaningful relationships and positive interactions.

Four pivotal skills—communication, interpersonal, negotiating, and conflict resolution—are at the heart of this chapter. We'll start with communication skills.

SUPERPOWER #13: COMMUNICATION SKILLS

Communication skills are the ability to clearly and effectively convey ideas, thoughts, and information to others. This superpower involves not only speaking or writing with clarity but also actively listening, interpreting nonverbal cues, and adapting your message to different audiences. It requires the ability to express oneself confidently while ensuring that the intended message is understood by the recipient. Mastering communication skills means being aware of tone, context, and audience needs, and using various mediums—such as verbal, written, or digital communication—appropriately and effectively.[1]

Wonder Woman's ability to express her ideas with clarity and conviction, whether she's speaking to world leaders or calming a tense situation, showcases the power of clear communication in building trust and resolving conflicts.

The Powers of Communication Skills

Unlocking the superpower of communication skills can profoundly enhance your life.[2] It helps you build strong, meaningful relationships by fostering trust and understanding. When you communicate effectively, you can resolve conflicts and prevent misunderstandings before they escalate. In academic and professional settings, the ability to clearly express your ideas—whether in essays, presentations, or discussions—leaves a lasting impression and creates more opportunities for growth and success.[3]

Persuasive communication allows you to influence others, whether you're leading a team, advocating for a cause, or negotiating a deal. Confidently expressing yourself boosts your self-assurance in conversations and presentations. When challenges arise, clear communication becomes a powerful tool, ensuring everyone involved understands the situation, reducing confusion and making problem-solving more efficient. By developing strong communication skills, you create a foundation for success and a more fulfilling life.[4]

At the heart of exceptional communication lie three fundamental pillars—effective expression, active listening, and nonverbal cues.

How to Wield This Superpower

Effective Expression

Effective expression involves conveying your thoughts, intentions, and emotions clearly. Here are some tips.[5]

- **Know your message.** Clarify what you want to communicate. If it's important, take time to plan what you want to say.
- **Consider your audience.** Tailor your message to suit your audience's understanding and emotional state. The language you choose for your teacher won't be the same as the language you would use with a close friend. Wonder Woman always tailors her communication based on the situation—whether using formal language in diplomatic discussions or connecting personally with those needing support. She adapts her tone and message to ensure her words resonate with the audience.
- **Structure your thoughts.** Organize your points logically with an introduction, body, and conclusion.
- **Be concise and direct.** Keep your message brief and to the point. The average attention span for people is 8.25 seconds, and although it can be up to 20 minutes, overall human attention span is decreasing.[6]

- **Check your audience for understanding.** Ask for feedback to ensure understanding and engagement.

By honing your ability to express yourself effectively, you can ensure your messages are clear and impactful and resonate with your audience, fostering better understanding and stronger connections.

Active Listening

Active listening[7] involves fully concentrating, understanding, responding to, and remembering what is being said. Key components include the following.

- **Give your full attention.** Focus entirely on the speaker by removing distractions like phones and items to fiddle with.
- **Show that you're listening.** Use verbal cues like "Yes" and "I see" and nonverbal cues like nodding and smiling.
- **Provide feedback.** Reflect on what has been said by paraphrasing, but only when they've finished talking—never interrupt.
- **Avoid making judgments.** Allow the speaker to finish before asking questions or offering ideas. Remember that sometimes a person just wants to talk, so ask if your opinion is wanted before offering it.
- **Respond appropriately.** Be candid and respectful in your responses, especially when communicating with people you're less familiar with.
- **Remember the information you're given.** Retain and recall what has been said.
- **Clarify and summarize.** Summarize what you've heard and ask questions to ensure understanding.

Active listening fosters better understanding, builds stronger relationships, and enhances your ability to respond thoughtfully and effectively in conversations.[8]

Nonverbal Cues

Nonverbal cues, which often convey more information than spoken words, include body language,[9] facial expressions, gestures, eye contact, posture, and tone of voice. Understanding these cues significantly enhances communication.

- **Facial expressions.** Convey emotions through your expressions.
- **Gestures.** Use hand movements to emphasize points.
- **Eye contact.** Show respect and interest with appropriate eye contact.
- **Posture and body orientation.** Use open and inviting body language.
- **Proximity.** Be mindful of personal space.
- **Tone of voice.** Adjust your tone to match your message.
- **Touch.** Use touch appropriately to communicate support or empathy.
- **Timing and pace.** Control the pace of your speech and the timing of your responses.[10]

Wonder Woman's confident stance and calm demeanor often speak louder than words, showing how nonverbal communication can enhance your message and inspire trust in those around you. By mastering nonverbal cues, you can enhance your communication, ensuring that your messages are more effective, empathetic, and aligned with your intentions.

Training Missions to Develop This Superpower

Engage in activities such as these to enhance your communication skills.

- **Join a debate club or public speaking group.** Improve verbal communication and self-expression.
- **Engage in role-playing games.** Practice different scenarios to enhance verbal and nonverbal communication.[11]
- **Play charades.** This is a great game to focus on body language to convey messages.
- **Volunteer for team leadership roles.** Take on roles that demand effective communication.
- **Be the conversation starter.** Ask family members how their day was or what the best and worst parts were. Use open-ended questions instead of those that lead to a yes or no answer.
- **Record and review personal presentations.** Self-assess and improve your delivery.
- **Watch and analyze speeches or performances.** Learn from skilled communicators.
- **Mute the TV.** See how much of a TV program you can follow without having the words to listen to.
- **Practice mindfulness and self-reflection.** Improve focus and self-awareness regarding interpersonal relations.
- **Pay attention to different cultures.** Learn about different verbal and nonverbal communication styles to prevent miscommunications in diverse environments.

In the 2017 film *Wonder Woman* starring Gal Gadot, Diana Prince exemplifies strong communication skills when she makes the bold decision to cross No Man's Land, despite the advice of others. Her conversation with Steve Trevor and the team is both clear and decisive. Diana passionately articulates her reasoning, not only leading through her actions but also by expressing her values and intentions with conviction. This direct communication inspires those around her to rally in support, ultimately leading to a crucial breakthrough on the battlefield. In this scene, Wonder Woman embodies assertiveness, clarity, and conviction—essential qualities for leadership and persuading others to follow.[12]

Action Items

- Before you read further, take a few minutes to consider the information presented in this section.
- Imagine yourself decades in the future (after decades of cultivating communication skills), and how you use this superpower to achieve your goals.
- Note how you currently employ this superpower in your daily life. Take pride in the progress you've already achieved in developing communication skills.
- Evaluate the effectiveness of your current practices to cultivate this superpower.
- If you decide that your current efforts to cultivate this superpower need to be improved, consider at least one improvement you can make in the coming weeks, months, or year.
- Develop a plan for implementing that improvement.

Now that we've addressed the superpower of communication skills, let's move on to interpersonal skills.

SUPERPOWER #14: INTERPERSONAL SKILLS

Interpersonal skills are the ability to interact effectively and harmoniously with others. This superpower involves understanding social dynamics, being aware of others' emotions and perspectives, and communicating in ways that foster positive relationships. It requires empathy, respect, and trust. Mastering interpersonal skills means navigating social situations with ease, adjusting to different personalities, and building strong connections through effective, meaningful interactions.[13]

The Powers of Interpersonal Skills and Empathy

Wonder Woman's ability to connect with people on a deep, personal level—whether in battle or negotiation—demonstrates how empathy and respect can foster collaboration and strengthen relationships.

Interpersonal skills also boost your emotional intelligence, increasing your self-awareness and helping you manage your reactions in social situations with greater ease and confidence. As you refine these abilities, doors to new opportunities—whether in jobs, leadership positions, or networking—naturally open up.

Furthermore, building positive relationships reduces loneliness, lowers stress levels, and increases your self-esteem and overall happiness. By honing your interpersonal skills, you set yourself up for stronger relationships, better communication, and greater well-being, paving the way for a more successful and fulfilling life.

Empathy, Respect, and Trust

At the core of interpersonal skills are three elements.[14]

- **Empathy.** Understanding and sharing another person's feelings creates genuine connections and deepens communication.[15]
- **Respect.** Recognizing everyone's inherent value fosters mutual appreciation, understanding, and constructive conflict resolution.[16]
- **Trust.** Built through consistent actions and integrity, trust allows for open ideas, risk-taking, and collaboration in a safe environment.[17]

Wonder Woman's empathy for others, whether comforting those in distress or mediating conflicts, shows that understanding another person's perspective is key to building meaningful, lasting connections. Empathy often serves as the foundational element, leading to respect and trust. These three elements uplift your interpersonal effectiveness, making you a better friend, collaborator, and leader.

How to Wield This Superpower

Here's a step-by-step process for mastering interpersonal skills.[18]

1. **Preparation.** Clear your mind of distractions, set your intentions, especially to eliminate any biases, and be present and attentive.
2. **Active listening.** Engage fully with the speaker through eye contact, nodding, and paraphrasing.
3. **Mindful observation.** Pay attention to nonverbal cues and body language to understand feelings and responses.

4. **Open communication.** Use 'I' statements to express thoughts and feelings openly and respectfully. This allows you to take ownership of your emotions so others don't feel they're being blamed for how you feel.
5. **Consistent integrity.** Be consistent and reliable in your actions to build credibility and trust. If you say you're going to do something, follow through.
6. **Reflective practice.** Reflect on interactions to understand others' perspectives and improve your approach.
7. **Continuous learning.** Engage in books, workshops, and educational opportunities to enhance empathy, respect, and trust, especially sources from different cultures.

Training Missions to Develop This Superpower

Engage in activities such as these to enhance your interpersonal skills.

- **Volunteer for a cause.** Community service exposes you to diverse groups, fostering empathy.
- **Join Model United Nations (MUN).** These platforms help you understand multiple viewpoints and practice respectful disagreements.[19]
- **Participate in team sports or group activities.** Working toward a common goal builds trust and dependability.
- **Model helpfulness and kindness.** Acts of helpfulness and kindness can improve connections and boost self-esteem.
- **Engage in cultural exchange programs.** Spending time in different cultural settings boosts empathy and respect.
- **Mentor or tutor peers.** Helping peers develops your trustworthiness and empathy while reinforcing your learning.

In the 2017 film *Wonder Woman*, Diana Prince exemplified interpersonal skills through her interactions with Steve Trevor's team, which includes characters like Charlie, Sameer, and The Chief. Despite coming from a background vastly different from theirs, Diana connects with each of them on a personal level. She listens with empathy, offers encouragement, and shows genuine interest in their stories, which helps her build trust and camaraderie. This ability to understand and relate to others' emotions and experiences is key to fostering strong relationships and is essential for teamwork and cooperation.[20]

Action Items

- Before you read further, take a few minutes to consider the information presented in this section.
- Imagine yourself decades in the future (after many years of cultivating interpersonal skills) and how you use this superpower to achieve your goals.
- Note how you currently employ interpersonal skills in your daily life. Take pride in the progress you've already achieved in developing this superpower.
- Evaluate the effectiveness of your current practices to cultivate interpersonal skills.
- If you decide that your current efforts to cultivate your interpersonal skills need to be improved, consider at least one improvement you can make in the coming weeks, months, or year.
- Develop a plan for implementing that improvement.

Now that we've addressed the superpower of interpersonal skills, let's move on to negotiating skills.

SUPERPOWER #15: NEGOTIATING SKILLS

Negotiating skills are the ability to engage in discussions to reach an agreement or compromise between two or more parties. This superpower involves understanding both sides' needs, desires, and goals while effectively communicating your own. It requires preparation, active listening, and the capacity to find common ground by proposing solutions that address all parties' interests. Mastering negotiating skills means navigating complex situations with tact, flexibility, and a focus on achieving mutually beneficial outcomes.[21]

Wonder Woman often uses her negotiating prowess to unite opposing sides in diplomatic talks or during conflicts.

The Powers of Negotiating Skills

Cultivating the superpower of negotiating skills can greatly enhance your ability to navigate both personal and professional situations. With strong negotiating skills, you can engage in productive discussions that help resolve conflicts and de-escalate tense situations, finding common ground that benefits everyone involved. By approaching negotiations with respect, empathy, and understanding, you build trust and foster goodwill, strengthening your relationships.[22]

Negotiation also sharpens your problem-solving abilities by encouraging you to consider multiple viewpoints and work collaboratively to develop solutions that address core concerns. Moreover, these skills help you prevent conflicts before they arise by seeking compromises and creating win-win outcomes, maintaining positive connections with others.

When you develop your negotiating skills, you gain the power to resolve conflicts peacefully, strengthen relationships, and create high-quality solutions that promote harmony and productivity in all areas of your life.[23]

How to Wield This Superpower

Here's a step-by-step process for mastering negotiating skills.

1. **Preparation.** Gather information and assess the situation before negotiating. Understand your goals and the other side's needs.
2. **Empathy.** Understand the perspectives and needs of those you're negotiating with. This is the time to ask the *why* behind their goals and needs.
3. **Communication.** Express your needs clearly and confidently and listen actively to gain insights into the other party's motivations.
4. **Flexibility.** Be open to different paths to achieve your goals, exploring alternatives without compromising your core values. Like Wonder Woman, who remains flexible in her approach to problem-solving during high-stakes negotiations, being adaptable helps you find creative solutions that benefit everyone involved.
5. **Silence.** Avoid filling moments of silence by overtalking, as this could make you look less confident.
6. **Assertiveness.** Express your thoughts and needs confidently and respectfully, ensuring your voice is heard and your boundaries are respected.
7. **Closure.** Conclude negotiations with clear terms and agreements. Reflect on the process to learn and improve for future negotiations.

8. **Trust.** Keep to your end of the negotiation to protect future relationships.[24]

Following these steps can enhance your negotiating skills, enabling you to achieve mutually beneficial outcomes and build stronger, more collaborative relationships.

Training Missions to Develop This Superpower

Engage in activities such as these to enhance your negotiating skills.

- **The family summit.** Initiate a family meeting to discuss a topic of mutual interest or contention. Prepare your case, practice empathy, assertiveness, and compromise, and reflect on the strategies used.
- **Bargain hunt.** Negotiate discounts or better deals at yard sales or flea markets. Practice persuasion and assertiveness in a low-stakes environment.
- **Role-playing games (RPGs).** Participate in games that require team strategy and negotiation. Develop critical thinking, empathy, and adaptability.[25]
- **Volunteer mediator.** Serve as a mediator in disputes among friends, schoolmates, or community groups. Develop active listening, empathy, and creative problem-solving skills.
- **Entrepreneurial ventures.** Start a small venture and negotiate prices, deadlines, and expectations with clients. Develop skills in articulating value and managing expectations.

- **Feedback forums.** Create or participate in forums to give and receive constructive criticism on negotiation encounters. Learn from others' experiences and refine your approach.

In the 2017 film *Wonder Woman*, Diana Prince showcases her negotiating skills during her confrontation with the British War Council. Though initially dismissed, she challenges their war strategy, advocating for a moral approach rather than simply accepting their tactics. Her persistence and unwavering commitment to doing what's right—insisting they cannot stand idly by while people suffer—ultimately make an impact. Diana's firm stance inspires Steve Trevor to act, illustrating that negotiation isn't always about compromise. Sometimes, it's about holding fast to your values while persuading others to recognize a broader, more ethical perspective.[26]

Action Items

- Before you read further, take a few minutes to consider the information presented in this section.
- Imagine yourself decades in the future (after many years of cultivating negotiating skills), and how you use this superpower to achieve your goals.
- Note how you currently employ negotiating skills in your daily life. Take pride in the progress you've already achieved in developing this superpower.
- Evaluate the effectiveness of your current practices to cultivate these skills.
- If you decide that your current efforts to cultivate negotiating skills need to be improved, consider at least one improvement you can make in the coming weeks, months, or year.

- Develop a plan for implementing that improvement.

Now that we've addressed the superpower of negotiating skills, let's move on to conflict resolution.

SUPERPOWER #16: CONFLICT RESOLUTION

Conflict resolution is the ability to constructively navigate and address disagreements or disputes between individuals or groups. This superpower involves identifying the root causes of conflicts, understanding the perspectives of all parties involved, and facilitating open, respectful communication to find a solution. It requires patience, empathy, and the skill to de-escalate tense situations while guiding others toward a common understanding or agreement. Mastering conflict resolution means mediating differences effectively and promoting harmony through collaborative problem-solving.[27]

Wonder Woman's ability to mediate conflicts with strength and compassion exemplifies how resolving disputes with empathy can create lasting peace and understanding.

The Powers of Conflict Resolution

Mastering the superpower of conflict resolution can profoundly impact your personal and professional life. It helps you foster emotional intelligence by enabling you to recognize, understand, and manage your own emotions while empathizing with others during tense situations. As you develop conflict resolution skills, you naturally enhance your communication abilities, learning how to actively listen, express your thoughts assertively, and clearly define your needs and boundaries.[28]

This skill also sharpens your problem-solving abilities by allowing you to identify the root causes of conflicts and work collaboratively toward solutions, expanding your critical and creative thinking in the process. Additionally, it builds resilience and adaptability, encouraging you to view conflicts as opportunities for growth and helping you face future challenges with greater confidence.

Finally, conflict resolution cultivates leadership qualities, empowering you to mediate disputes, inspire teamwork, and foster a culture of respect. By mastering this skill, you equip yourself with the tools needed to create a more harmonious, resilient, and successful life.[29]

How to Wield This Superpower

Here's a step-by-step process for mastering conflict resolution.[30]

1. **Embrace calmness as your shield.** Stay calm by taking slow, deep breaths. A calm mind is crucial in the heat of conflict.
2. **Listen with the intent to understand.** Engage in active listening without planning your response. Notice body language, tone, and emotions.
3. **Communicate your feelings without assigning blame.** Use "I" statements to express your feelings without putting the other person on the defensive.
4. **Seek common ground.** Look for areas of agreement or empathy. Sometimes, agreeing to disagree respectfully can create mutual understanding.
5. **Collaborate on a solution.** Work together to find a resolution that respects both sides. Brainstorm solutions and forge a path forward.

6. **Seek help when needed.** Recognize when to seek assistance from a mediator, counselor, or trusted adult for complex conflicts.
7. **Reflect and learn.** Reflect on what you learned about yourself and others. Consider what you could do differently next time to improve conflict management.

By incorporating these steps, you can master conflict resolution, transforming disputes into opportunities for growth and understanding while fostering healthier relationships.

Training Missions to Develop This Superpower

Engage in activities such as these to enhance your conflict-resolution skills.

- **Role-playing scenarios.** Practice conflict resolution in controlled environments by acting out disagreements with friends, family, or teachers.[31]
- **Peer mediation training.** Participate in peer mediation programs to facilitate productive discussions and help others reach agreements.
- **Communication workshops.** Attend workshops focused on assertive communication, nonverbal cues, and the importance of tone in resolving conflicts.
- **Emotional intelligence development.** Engage in mindfulness exercises, journaling, and empathy-building games to manage emotions better.
- **Collaborative group projects.** Work on group projects that require negotiation, compromise, and collaboration. Wonder Woman frequently works alongside others to craft solutions that respect the values of everyone

involved, demonstrating the importance of collaboration in finding lasting resolutions.

- **Debate clubs or public speaking groups.** Join a debate club or public speaking group to sharpen your ability to articulate arguments and consider opposing viewpoints.
- **Volunteering in community service.** Broaden your perspectives and enhance empathy through real-world conflicts and challenges in community service.

In the 2017 film *Wonder Woman,* Diana Prince demonstrates her conflict resolution skills during her battle with Ares. She faces not only a physical clash but a profound moral dilemma. Ares attempts to persuade her that humanity is inherently evil and deserves destruction. Rather than simply engaging in combat, Diana reflects on her own experiences with people, ultimately resolving the conflict within herself. She chooses love and compassion over vengeance, reaffirming her belief in humanity's potential for good. This decision not only resolves the immediate conflict but also solidifies her guiding principle that true conflict resolution involves more than external battles—it requires inner clarity, staying true to one's values, and choosing a path that fosters peace and understanding.[32]

Action Items

- Before you read further, take a few minutes to consider the information presented in this section.
- Imagine yourself decades in the future (after many years of cultivating conflict resolution) and how you use this superpower to achieve your goals.
- Note how you currently employ conflict resolution in your daily life. Take pride in the progress you've already achieved in developing this superpower.

- Evaluate the effectiveness of your current practices to cultivate conflict resolution.
- If you decide that your current efforts to cultivate these skills need to be improved, consider at least one improvement you can make in the coming weeks, months, or year.
- Develop a plan for implementing that improvement.

As we conclude this chapter on communication and interpersonal skills, let's revisit the inspiring example of Wonder Woman. She teaches us the profound impact of skilled communication, empathy, and understanding in leading and uniting individuals from diverse backgrounds. Just as Wonder Woman leverages her gifts for the greater good, so can you harness your communication and interpersonal skills to lead with empathy, respect, and trust, transforming challenges into opportunities for growth and unity.

What Does Superhero Mean to You?

Is it about a cape and saving the day or is it about using the powers you have to make a difference?

"Being the best you can be, that's doable. That's possible for anybody if they put their mind to it."[1]

— CAPTAIN MARVEL

As we reach the halfway point, it's become clear that you are a superhero in your own right. Through sleep, diet, exercise, and stress management, you have physical and mental power. With analytical thinking and decision-making, you have mental power. And with EQ, you have emotional power.

All this power will make your dreams and ambitions a reality. You're well on your way to actually enjoying your teen years— which is what you should be doing.

But remember the concerns mentioned at the beginning of this book. Far too many teens are struggling with anxiety and depression, as well as other mental health conditions. They can't cope with the immense pressure they are under, and they feel alone.

It's heartbreaking that many of those teens have reached a point where they don't think life is worth living.

You have another hidden superpower—the power to help them— even if they are strangers!

These teens feel they have no place to turn for help finding the solutions they need to turn their lives around.

By sharing your opinions of this book on Amazon, teens who desperately want to find their inner strengths can see that there is a solution for them too. Your words have incredible power.

Let's break barriers, let's be there for each other, and let's make the future a brighter place for everyone with a new generation of superheroes. Thank you in advance because I know you can make a difference!

Scan the QR code below:

In the next chapter, we'll explore how embracing leadership, emotional intelligence, teamwork, and responsible citizenship can further empower you to become a real-life superhero.

LEADERSHIP AND TEAMWORK

Drawing inspiration from Captain America, a leadership figure within the Marvel Universe, we can extract valuable lessons.[1] His exemplary attributes—from emotional intelligence and the ability to blend with diverse personalities to his unwavering commitment and sense of duty—serve as an example for aspiring leaders, demonstrating that effective leadership surpasses the boundaries of age and formal titles.[2]

This chapter is for aspiring leaders and team players who envision leaving a mark on the world. We'll delve into the strategic life skills of leadership, emotional intelligence, teamwork, and responsible citizenship, each an essential component in a young visionary's toolbox.

Leadership and teamwork are the superpowers that, when mastered, can transform your dreams into reality. We'll begin with leadership skills.

SUPERPOWER #17: LEADERSHIP SKILLS

Leadership skills are the ability to guide, inspire, and influence others toward achieving a common goal. This superpower involves setting a positive example, providing clear direction, and motivating individuals or teams to perform at their best. It requires effective communication, decision-making, and the ability to assess situations and delegate responsibilities. Mastering leadership skills means understanding how to bring out the strengths of others, manage challenges, and foster an environment where collaboration and growth can thrive.[3]

Captain America's leadership shines not just because of his strength but because of his ability to inspire others to unite for a common cause, even when the odds seem impossible.

The Powers of Leadership Skills

Strengthening your leadership skills can significantly elevate the quality of your life. As a leader, you gain the ability to make informed decisions by analyzing situations, weighing options, and anticipating outcomes. This not only strengthens your decision-making but also enhances your self-confidence as you successfully guide projects and inspire others. Your communication skills will improve, as effective leadership requires you to articulate your ideas clearly and listen actively to the perspectives of others.

Leadership also teaches the value of collaboration, helping you unite people from diverse backgrounds toward a shared goal. You'll develop a strong sense of responsibility and accountability, building your credibility both personally and professionally. Additionally, leadership opens doors to new opportunities by expanding your network, allowing you to connect with peers, mentors, and influencers who can help shape your future.

By navigating challenges and solving problems, you build resilience, which is essential for overcoming obstacles and staying adaptable. Ultimately, by mastering leadership skills, you set yourself on a path toward a successful and impactful life, empowering yourself to make a difference.

Leadership by Example

Leading by example means modeling the behaviors, attitudes, and work ethic you want others to follow. When you lead by example, you demonstrate the standards you expect, showing rather than telling others what is important. This approach is about integrity and consistency—doing what you say and setting a positive precedent for others to emulate. People are more likely to trust and respect a leader who practices what they preach. In your role, focus on showing dedication, being accountable, and treating others with respect to inspire those around you to do the same.[4]

Positive Reinforcement

Positive reinforcement is a strategy used to encourage desired behavior by rewarding it. When you use positive reinforcement, you give praise, recognition, or other rewards immediately after someone does something well. This approach reinforces that behavior, making it more likely to be repeated. In your role, look for opportunities to acknowledge good work and progress, no matter how small, because it motivates others and builds their confidence. Whether it's offering a compliment, giving a high-five, or just saying "well done," positive reinforcement is a powerful tool for building a supportive and motivated environment.[5]

How to Wield This Superpower

Effectively using the superpower of leadership involves a structured approach that blends clear vision, communication, and support.[6]

- **Goals and values.** Define your goals and values. This will provide a strong foundation and help you make decisions that align with your purpose.
- **Vision.** Communicate your vision clearly to those you lead. Ensure everyone understands what the team is working toward and why it matters.
- **Lead by example.** Be the first to show up, work hard, and hold yourself to the same standards you set for others.
- **Positive reinforcement.** Use positive reinforcement to recognize efforts and progress, making it clear that contributions are valued. Stay calm and focused when challenges arise, guiding others through with encouragement rather than criticism.
- **Feedback and adjustment.** Regularly seek feedback and adjust your approach based on what you learn.

By following this process, you'll build trust, inspire others, and create an environment where everyone feels motivated to contribute and succeed.[7]

Training Missions to Develop This Superpower

Engage in activities such as these to enhance your leadership skills.

- **Start a club.** Find some people with a shared interest or take on a leadership role in school clubs.

- **Identify strengths and weaknesses.** Not just your own but the whole group, so you know where you can support each other.
- **Practice public speaking.** Improve your speaking skills through classes or clubs.
- **Organize an event.** Plan and execute events like fundraisers, community clean-ups, and sports competitions to develop your organizational abilities.
- **Participate in student government.** Gain practical leadership experience through associations, unions, and houses.
- **Become a networking pro.** Take advantage of professional sites like LinkedIn and out-of-school clubs and societies to meet leader role models.
- **Consider internships.** Internships give you invaluable experience with problem-solving, communication, and proactive learning.[8]

In the 2014 film *Captain America: The Winter Soldier*, during the climactic battle, Captain America (Steve Rogers) leads a critical mission to stop Hydra from using S.H.I.E.L.D.'s helicarriers to carry out mass eliminations. Despite facing overwhelming odds, Steve steps up, delivering an inspiring speech to the S.H.I.E.L.D. agents, urging them to stand up for what is right. He clearly outlines the plan and motivates his team to take action, even at great personal risk. This scene showcases Captain America's leadership by example, as he not only inspires others to follow a moral path but also ensures that everyone understands their role in the mission, fostering a united effort.[9]

Action Items

- Before you read further, take a few minutes to consider the information presented in this section.
- Imagine yourself decades in the future (after many years of cultivating leadership skills) and how you use this superpower to achieve your goals.
- Note how you currently employ these skills in your daily life. Take pride in the progress you've already achieved in developing leadership skills.
- Evaluate the effectiveness of your current practices to cultivate this superpower.
- If you decide that your current efforts to cultivate leadership skills need to be improved, consider at least one improvement you can make in the coming weeks, months, or year.
- Develop a plan for implementing that improvement.

Now that we've addressed the superpower of leadership skills, let's move on to emotional intelligence.

SUPERPOWER #18: EMOTIONAL INTELLIGENCE

Emotional intelligence, EQ, is the ability to recognize, understand, and manage your own emotions while also being attuned to the emotions of others. This superpower involves self-awareness, empathy, and emotional regulation, allowing you to navigate social interactions with sensitivity and understanding. It requires the ability to identify emotional cues in yourself and others, respond appropriately to emotional situations, and maintain balance in emotionally charged circumstances. Mastering emotional intelligence means developing strong relationships, managing stress, and adapting to emotional dynamics with awareness and control.[10]

Captain America's emotional intelligence enables him to stay calm in high-pressure situations, read the emotions of his teammates, and offer the empathy and understanding needed to bring them together.

The Powers of Emotional Intelligence

Enhancing your emotional intelligence can transform the way you interact with others and navigate your own emotions. By developing self-awareness, you gain the ability to understand your strengths and weaknesses, recognize emotional triggers, and regulate your responses. This not only helps you manage stress and difficult situations but also earns the trust and respect of your peers, as they see you leading by example.

Empathy, another key component of emotional intelligence, allows you to truly understand and appreciate different perspectives. This makes you better equipped to handle complex team dynamics and build meaningful connections with those around you. Effective communication flows naturally from emotional intelligence, helping you clearly convey your ideas, expectations, and concerns. You become skilled at resolving conflicts, finding common ground, and fostering understanding in both personal and group settings.

Emotional intelligence also enhances your ability to work within teams. You'll lead with compassion, negotiate with empathy, and resolve disagreements with grace, which fosters a sense of camaraderie and mutual respect. In leadership, emotional intelligence transforms your approach from one of authority to one of influence and inspiration, enabling you to build close-knit, thriving teams that are motivated by your example.

In mastering emotional intelligence, you sharpen your abilities in self-awareness, empathy, communication, teamwork, and leadership. This superpower equips you to build strong, lasting relationships, inspire those around you, and tackle life's challenges with confidence and poise.[11]

How to Wield This Superpower

There are five core elements to EQ: self-awareness, self-regulation, motivation, empathy, and social skills.[12]

1. **Self-awareness.** Know your emotions by paying attention to how you feel in different situations and identifying triggers. Keep a journal to track and reflect on your emotions.
2. **Self-regulation.** Control your responses without suppressing feelings. Use techniques like deep breathing to stay composed. Picture your emotions in the third person, separate from you, to create distance.
3. **Motivation.** Channel your emotions positively toward your goals. Use passion to drive you forward. Set clear, attainable goals with rewards for each step you achieve.
4. **Empathy.** Understand others' emotions by putting yourself in their shoes. Listen actively and show genuine interest in their feelings and concerns. Avoid the phrase "I know how you feel" unless you really do. Captain America's empathy allows him to connect deeply with those around him, whether it's comforting a struggling team member or understanding the motivations of his allies and adversaries alike.

5. **Social skills.** Build strong relationships through clear communication, awareness of nonverbal cues, and effective conflict resolution. Observe environments and adjust your communication style to suit your audience.

With these steps, emotional intelligence allows you to navigate personal and social complexities while building stronger, more empathetic relationships.

Training Missions to Develop This Superpower

There's just one training mission here—self-reflection on your emotional intelligence. Consider using a journal, notepad, or digital document on your phone or laptop to complete these journal prompts.[13]

- How do you feel right now?
- What emotions have you experienced throughout the day?
- What made you feel grateful today?
- When was the last time you felt genuinely happy?
- What's going well in your life now?
- What could be better for you?
- What does anger feel like to you?
- What do you do when you feel angry?
- What was the last thing that made you cry?
- If your friend made a mistake, what advice would you give them?
- Who can you talk about your emotions with?
- How do you feel when people misunderstand you?
- What do you need to do to let go of any regrets you have?

In the 2016 film *Captain America: Civil War,* when the Avengers are divided over the Sokovia Accords, Steve Rogers exemplifies emotional intelligence by acknowledging and respecting the differing opinions within the team. While he firmly opposes the Accords, Steve listens to Tony Stark's perspective, understanding the guilt and sense of responsibility driving Tony's stance. Despite the escalating conflict, Steve remains composed, demonstrating empathy for his teammates' emotional states while staying true to his own principles. His ability to manage both his own emotions and those of others in high-pressure situations highlights his emotional intelligence, enabling him to maintain relationships and effectively navigate the complex dynamics of the team.[14]

Action Items

- Before you read further, take a few minutes to consider the information presented in this section.
- Imagine yourself decades in the future (after many years of cultivating emotional intelligence), and how you use this superpower to achieve your goals.
- Note how you currently employ emotional intelligence in your daily life. Take pride in the progress you've already achieved in developing this superpower.
- Evaluate the effectiveness of your current practices to cultivate emotional intelligence.
- If you decide that your current efforts to cultivate these skills need to be improved, consider at least one improvement you can make in the coming weeks, months, or year.
- Develop a plan for implementing that improvement.

Now that we've addressed the superpower of emotional intelligence, let's move on to teamwork.

SUPERPOWER #19: TEAMWORK

Teamwork is the collaborative effort of a group of individuals working together toward a common goal or objective. It involves effective communication, mutual respect, cooperation, and the ability to leverage the diverse strengths of team members. Successful teamwork requires individuals to set aside personal agendas, trust one another, and contribute their skills to achieve shared success, often resulting in more innovative solutions and better outcomes than could be accomplished alone.[15]

Captain America's ability to rally diverse groups—whether it's his fellow Avengers or a band of soldiers—highlights how teamwork thrives when everyone's unique strengths are valued and directed toward a common goal.

The Powers of Teamwork

Gaining proficiency in teamwork can have a transformative effect on your life in diverse ways. By working with others, you gain access to diverse perspectives, which leads to more creative and effective problem-solving. Tasks are completed more efficiently when you divide responsibilities based on individual strengths, allowing the team to accomplish more in less time.

Teamwork also provides countless learning opportunities, as you can absorb valuable insights from your teammates' experiences and skills. It creates a built-in support system where members encourage and assist each other, which is especially important during challenging projects. Regular communication within a team improves your ability to express your ideas clearly and listen to others, sharpening your overall communication skills.

Being part of a team fosters a sense of accountability and responsibility. You not only become accountable to the group but also develop trust and reliability. It's also a great environment to practice leadership, whether you take on a formal leadership role or lead by influence, helping you refine your leadership skills.

Navigating conflicts that arise in teamwork allows you to build conflict resolution skills, enabling you to handle disputes with maturity and understanding. Completing a project successfully with a team brings a sense of shared accomplishment, deepening your connection with others. Plus, teamwork helps you build a valuable network of peers and mentors, contributing to both your career and personal growth.

Mastering teamwork will elevate your ability to collaborate, communicate, and lead, all of which are essential for achieving long-term success.[16]

How to Wield This Superpower

Here's a step-by-step process for mastering teamwork.

1. **Assemble your team.** Gather a diverse group of individuals with different skills, perspectives, and strengths.
2. **Define a clear goal.** Ensure everyone understands the mission. Having a clear, shared goal provides direction and purpose.
3. **Assign roles and responsibilities.** Identify each member's strengths and assign roles to prevent overlap and foster accountability.

4. **Encourage open communication.** Lead by example with open, honest dialogue. Regular check-ins help ensure that everyone stays on the same page and that any issues are addressed promptly.

5. **Build trust and respect.** Show appreciation for contributions and respect opinions. Trust is earned through reliability and consistency.

6. **Embrace collaboration.** Work together to brainstorm ideas, solve problems, and make decisions. Encourage a collaborative environment. Just like Captain America brings out the best in his teammates by encouraging open communication and respecting their input, successful teams harness the power of collaboration to achieve greater things together.

7. **Navigate conflicts constructively.** Address conflicts head-on, focusing on solutions rather than blame. Avoid talking about others behind their backs.

8. **Celebrate achievements.** Recognizing and celebrating successes boosts morale and reinforces a positive team culture.

By following these steps, you can create a cohesive and effective group dynamic that leverages diverse strengths and fosters a collaborative and supportive environment.[17]

Training Missions to Develop This Superpower

Engage in activities such as these to enhance your teamwork prowess.

- **Join a sports team.** Participate in team-based activities to learn communication, strategy, and support. Notice how your coach uses each player's strengths.

- **Participate in theater productions or music bands.** Arts require cooperation and trust, as well as teaching patience and appreciation for collective effort.
- **Organize group study sessions.** Share knowledge and challenge concepts collaboratively to achieve academic goals.
- **Start a collaborative community project.** Initiate a project with friends, set shared goals, manage conflicts, and celebrate successes as you make improvements to your local area.
- **Embark on team-based adventure sports or activities.** Activities like rock climbing or escape rooms require trust, communication, and problem-solving as a group.
- **Plan a day trip.** With your parents' permission, plan a trip to a new place so that you can practice your skills in different environments outside of your usual comfort zone.
- **Don't cherry-pick your projects.** Don't just choose the projects you like to work on as a team. Suggest team projects and accept invitations.

In the 2012 film *The Avengers*, during the Battle of New York, Captain America works seamlessly with his fellow Avengers to defend the city against the Chitauri invasion. Demonstrating his ability to quickly assess each team member's strengths, he efficiently coordinates their efforts, assigning roles that maximize the team's effectiveness. For example, he directs Iron Man to contain the perimeter and Hulk to handle the heaviest firepower. This scene underscores Captain America's exceptional teamwork skills, as he leads by example and fosters collaboration, ensuring the team's combined efforts result in success.[18]

Action Items

- Before you read further, take a few minutes to consider the information presented in this section.
- Imagine yourself decades in the future (after many years of cultivating teamwork), and how you use this superpower to achieve your goals.
- Note how you currently employ teamwork in your daily life. Take pride in the progress you've already achieved in developing this superpower.
- Evaluate the effectiveness of your current practices to cultivate these skills.
- If you decide that your current efforts to cultivate teamwork need to be improved, consider at least one improvement you can make in the coming weeks, months, or year.
- Develop a plan for implementing that improvement.

Now that we've addressed the superpower of teamwork, let's move on to responsible citizenship.

SUPERPOWER #20: RESPONSIBLE CITIZENSHIP

Responsible citizenship is the practice of actively contributing to the well-being of one's community and society by upholding ethical standards, respecting laws, and promoting positive social change. It involves being informed about local and global issues, participating in civic duties such as voting, volunteering, and advocating for justice, and demonstrating respect for others. Responsible citizens are accountable for their actions, engage in civic activities, promote the common good, and obey the law.[19]

Captain America's unwavering commitment to justice and protecting the greater good makes him the ultimate role model for responsible citizenship, showing that leadership is about serving others and standing up for what's right.

The Powers of Responsible Citizenship

Developing the superpower of responsible citizenship can deeply enrich your life and the lives of those around you. By actively engaging in your community, you build a strong sense of belonging, which can enhance your mental health and overall well-being. Developing empathy and ethical values through exposure to diverse perspectives helps you make thoughtful, informed decisions that consider the needs of others.[20]

When you take initiative in community projects, you not only build leadership skills but also position yourself as a role model, demonstrating the kind of leadership that transcends personal gain and benefits the collective. Tackling complex social and economic issues sharpens your critical thinking and problem-solving abilities, equipping you to navigate challenges in all areas of life.

Responsible citizenship also opens doors to networking with people from diverse backgrounds and professions, creating mentorship opportunities and building relationships that can positively impact your career. Colleges and employers value applicants who demonstrate a commitment to their communities, making your dedication to citizenship a standout quality.

Engaging in local governance empowers you to have a voice in decisions that shape your community, giving you the opportunity to influence positive change. Additionally, by staying informed on global issues, you contribute to building a better world. Personal fulfillment comes from knowing that your actions make a tangible difference, and the civic skills you develop—such as advocacy, public speaking, and organizing—will benefit you throughout your life.

By mastering responsible citizenship, you gain the tools to create meaningful change in your community and beyond, while building valuable skills that will serve you well into the future.[21]

How to Wield This Superpower

Here's a step-by-step process for mastering responsible citizenship.

1. **Educate yourself.** Stay informed about issues affecting your community, your nation, and the world. Read news from multiple sources, engage with diverse perspectives, and keep updated on current events.
2. **Get involved.** Volunteer for local organizations, join clubs focused on civic engagement, and attend community meetings. Your involvement, no matter how small, can have a significant impact.
3. **Vote wisely.** When you reach voting age, use your vote as a tool for change. Research candidates and their policies thoroughly before casting your ballot.
4. **Uphold the law.** Respect and follow the laws of your community and country. Advocate for justice and fairness, support reforms for unjust laws, and ensure your actions do not harm others.
5. **Advocate for change.** Use your voice to advocate for causes you believe in. Write letters to elected officials, participate in peaceful protests, and use social media to raise awareness. Captain America never hesitates to

advocate for change when he believes something is wrong, reminding us that responsible citizens must sometimes challenge the status quo to create a better future.

6. **Respect others.** Treat everyone with respect and kindness, regardless of their background or beliefs. Stand against discrimination and injustice.

7. **Stay informed and adapt.** Continuous learning and flexibility are key components of responsible citizenship. Stay informed about new developments and be willing to adapt your actions and attitudes.

8. **Mentor and inspire others.** Share your knowledge and experiences with others, especially younger individuals. Be a role model in your community, demonstrating the values and behaviors of a responsible citizen.

By following these steps, you can master responsible citizenship, positively impacting your community and beyond while promoting justice and respect for all.[22]

Training Missions to Develop This Superpower

Engage in activities such as these to enhance responsible citizenship.[23]

- **Walk dogs for the elderly or neighbors who are incapable.** Offer to take their pets for a walk, provide companionship for the pets, and help neighbors who may have difficulty doing it themselves.
- **Visit the elderly or infirm neighbors.** Chat with them, read to them, or keep them company. Your presence and conversation can brighten their day.

- **Prepare or serve meals at a local soup kitchen.** Volunteer to help prepare and serve meals to those in need, practicing compassion.
- **Help younger students with homework.** Offer assistance to younger students who need help with homework or understanding a subject, aiding their academic success.
- **Grocery shop for the elderly or sick.** Reach out to someone in your community and offer to do their grocery shopping, assisting those who may have difficulty going to the store.
- **Help an older person with technology.** Assist older adults in navigating computers, smartphones, or other devices, bridging the generation gap with patience and knowledge.
- **Provide free childcare to family members or friends.** Offer childcare assistance, giving them a break while ensuring the safety and care of the children.
- **Fundraise for a cause you care about.** Organize a fundraiser to raise awareness and funds for a cause you're passionate about, engaging friends, family, and the community.
- **Help at an animal shelter.** Volunteer at a local animal shelter, assisting with tasks like walking dogs, feeding animals, cleaning cages, or fundraising.[24]

In the 2011 film *Captain America: The First Avenger*, even before gaining his superpowers, Steve Rogers exemplifies responsible citizenship by persistently attempting to enlist in the military during World War II, despite being repeatedly rejected due to his physical limitations. Motivated by a deep sense of duty, Steve is determined to serve and protect his country, famously declaring, "I don't like bullies—I don't care where they're from." His unwavering desire to fight for justice, even without powers, defines his strong sense of civic responsibility. This situation underscores

Steve's belief that leadership isn't about power—it's about standing up for others and contributing to the greater good, a principle that guides him throughout his journey.[25]

Action Items

- Before you read further, take a few minutes to consider the information presented in this section.
- Imagine yourself decades in the future (after many years of cultivating responsible citizenship), and how you are using this superpower to achieve your goals.
- Note how you currently employ these skills in your daily life. Take pride in the progress you've already achieved in developing responsible citizenship.
- Evaluate the effectiveness of your current practices to cultivate these skills.
- If you decide that your current efforts to cultivate responsible citizenship need to be improved, consider at least one improvement you can make in the coming weeks, months, or year.
- Develop a plan for implementing that improvement.

Captain America exemplifies the superpowers of leadership, emotional intelligence, teamwork, and responsible citizenship. His leadership is not just about being at the forefront of battles but also about connecting deeply with his teammates, fostering unity and trust through empathy. By respecting each team member's unique strengths and using them toward a shared goal, he shows that teamwork is more than collaboration—it's about valuing differences. His unwavering commitment to justice and service highlights that leadership is about uplifting others and making ethical choices. Captain America's story demonstrates that these traits are interconnected and accessible to anyone willing to embrace them, inspiring us to strive for greatness in ourselves and our communities.[26]

Having explored leadership, emotional intelligence, teamwork, and responsible citizenship, let's now focus on mastering practical life management.

PRACTICAL LIFE MANAGEMENT

This chapter introduces the core elements of practical life management—where the art of habit and routine, the science of time management, the precision of information management, the strategy of money management, and the foresight of career planning intersect. Mastering these skills lays the foundation for a life defined by growth, fulfillment, and excellence.

Think of Black Widow, a superhero whose success isn't just a result of her combat abilities, but of her exceptional talent for balancing complex aspects of her life with skill and precision—an embodiment of practical life management at its best.[1]

Let's begin with habit and routine management.

SUPERPOWER #21: HABIT AND ROUTINE MANAGEMENT

Habits and routines are often confused because they seem so similar—after all, routines frequently include habits. But understanding the difference between the two is key to managing your day effectively. Let's break them down and see what sets them apart.

- *Habits* are actions or behaviors that are repeated regularly and tend to occur subconsciously. They are developed through repetition over time, becoming automatic responses to certain cues or triggers. Examples include brushing your teeth every morning or checking your phone as soon as you wake up. Once they're ingrained, habits often require minimal thought.[2]
- *Routines* are more deliberate sets of actions performed in a specific sequence to achieve a desired outcome. While they can eventually become habitual, routines usually involve conscious planning and decision-making. An example is a morning routine that includes exercising, showering, and making breakfast. Unlike habits, routines require active effort and are often more structured.[3]

Both habits and routines are essential for effective habit and routine management, helping individuals maintain consistency and structure in their daily lives.

Black Widow's disciplined lifestyle shows the power of maintaining strong habits and routines. Her commitment to daily training ensures she's always ready for any challenge.

The Powers of Habit and Routine Management

Harnessing the superpower of habit and routine management can significantly enhance your life, personally and professionally. When you develop structured behavior patterns, you naturally become more consistent, reliable, and resilient, qualities that others will trust and respect. By creating routines, you're also improving your ability to manage time and boost productivity, as you'll be able to prioritize tasks more effectively and allocate time where it's needed most.

This skill helps build self-discipline, as sticking to habits requires focus and perseverance, especially when distractions arise. Consistent routines strengthen your willpower, making it easier to stay on track toward your goals. Habit and routine management also play a vital role in supporting your mental health. Having a predictable structure in your day brings stability, which can be especially helpful during stressful or uncertain times.[4]

Finally, this superpower encourages personal growth and self-improvement. Regularly assessing and refining your routines ensures that your habits stay aligned with your evolving goals and values. This leads to a more balanced, structured, and fulfilling life.

Routines

A well-structured routine is like a blueprint for your day, outlining where your time and energy will be directed. Routines are a collection of linked habits and actions organized into a specific sequence to help you achieve a consistent outcome. Think of routines as a way to automate your life so you can focus on more complex goals and ambitions.

Components of a Routine

- **Trigger or cue.** Each routine starts with a trigger—a signal that prompts you to begin the sequence. This could be waking up, arriving at school, or finishing homework.

- **Actions or habits.** These are the behaviors performed in a specific order. For example, a morning routine might include stretching, brushing your teeth, eating breakfast, and reviewing your daily goals.
- **Sequence and timing.** Routines are about the order and duration of actions. Having a consistent structure is crucial, but it should also be flexible enough to adjust when necessary.
- **Purpose or outcome.** Every routine should be designed with a purpose, such as optimizing your morning, enhancing focus before a study session, or unwinding before sleep.

Creating Effective Routines

To build a solid routine, follow this step-by-step process.

1. **Define your purpose.** Identify what you want the routine to accomplish. Is it to improve productivity, maintain focus, or care for your physical health? Write down the goal so you have a clear target.
2. **List the actions.** Break down each action needed to achieve that purpose. Start with the essential habits and add in supportive actions. For example, a study routine could include clearing your desk, reviewing your notes, setting a timer, and taking breaks.
3. **Order and optimize.** Arrange these actions in a logical sequence. Group similar activities together to save time, and think about the best order to maintain momentum. For instance, physical activities like stretching or exercise should come before mentally demanding tasks like problem-solving.

4. **Set time blocks.** Assign a realistic amount of time to each action. This helps prevent procrastination and ensures you're not rushing through the routine. For example, if you're creating a morning routine, set aside enough time to complete it without feeling rushed.

5. **Create a trigger.** Choose a consistent trigger that will cue your routine to start. This could be a specific time of day or an event, like getting home from school or hearing your alarm clock ring.

6. **Test and adjust.** Implement the routine for a week and observe how it fits into your life. Are some actions taking longer than expected? Do you feel more focused or stressed? Adjust the sequence, time blocks, or specific actions based on what's working or needs improvement.

7. **Refine and repeat.** Routines should evolve over time. As your priorities change, update your routines to reflect new goals or interests. Regularly refining your routines keeps them effective and aligned with your long-term vision.

By following this process, you can create routines that serve your goals and reduce decision fatigue, helping you stay on track even when life gets busy.

How to Form a New Habit

Forming a new habit can feel like unlocking a superpower within yourself, one that transforms small daily actions into a routine that serves your long-term goals. Here's a process to help you develop any new habit, step by step.[5]

1. **Start with a Clear Intention.** Decide on a specific habit you want to develop. Instead of saying, "I want to exercise more," say, "I will walk for 30 minutes every day after

school." By being clear and specific, you give your brain a simple target to focus on.

2. **Anchor It to an Existing Routine.** To make this new habit stick, connect it to something you already do daily. For example, if you want to practice mindfulness, tie it to brushing your teeth each morning. You could say to yourself, "After I brush my teeth, I will spend five minutes in mindfulness." Linking your new habit to a routine you already have makes it easier to remember and follow through.

3. **Start Small and Be Consistent.** It's tempting to go big, but lasting habits are built by consistency, not size. If you want to read more, start with just ten minutes daily. The key is making the habit easy enough to do it daily, no matter what. Remember, the goal is to show up consistently—even when you don't feel like it.

4. **Use a Trigger and Reward System.** Set up a system that reminds you to do the habit (the trigger) and rewards you when you complete it. For example, if your habit is studying for 20 minutes after dinner, the act of finishing dinner is your trigger. Once you've completed your study session, reward yourself with something simple, like listening to your favorite song. The trigger-reward loop reinforces the habit in your brain, making it easier to repeat.

5. **Track Your Progress.** Use a journal, a habit-tracking app, or a simple calendar to mark each day you successfully complete your habit. Tracking your progress helps you see how far you've come and motivates you to keep going. There's power in watching a streak build up, and it pushes you to avoid breaking the chain.

6. **Be Patient and Adjust as Needed.** It takes time to build a new habit, so be patient with yourself. If you miss a day, don't be discouraged—just pick up where you left off. If the habit isn't sticking, adjust it. Maybe you need to simplify it or shift the time of day when you do it. Stay flexible and committed, knowing that every small step counts.[6]

By following these steps, you'll transform the act of forming a new habit into a superpower you can use to build the life you want.

How to Break a Bad Habit

Breaking a bad habit can feel like taking back control over your actions, allowing you to direct your energy toward more positive, empowering behaviors. Here's a process that can help you successfully break a bad habit.[7]

1. **Identify the Habit and Its Triggers.** The first step in breaking a bad habit is to recognize it clearly. Be specific about the habit you want to stop, whether it's procrastination, biting your nails, or excessive screen time. Then, take a closer look at what triggers the habit. Do you tend to procrastinate when you're stressed, or reach for your phone out of boredom? Understanding the situations, emotions, or environments that lead to the habit will help you gain control over it.

2. **Replace the Habit with a Positive Action.** Instead of just focusing on stopping the habit, think about what you can do instead. It's easier to replace a bad habit with a good one than to simply stop altogether. If you want to cut down on mindless snacking, for example, you could replace it with drinking water or going for a short walk

when you feel the urge. The key is to swap the negative behavior for something that supports your well-being.

3. **Make It Hard to Continue the Habit.** One of the most effective ways to break a habit is to make it difficult to keep doing it. If your bad habit is spending too much time on social media, try deleting the apps from your phone or setting strict time limits. If it's eating junk food, don't keep it in the house. By making the habit less convenient, you'll reduce the chances of slipping back into it.

4. **Use Reminders to Stay on Track.** You can't rely on willpower alone to break a bad habit. Set up reminders to help you stay on course. These could be notes or alarms that remind you of your goal, or even a friend or family member who can help hold you accountable. For example, if you're trying to stop overspending, leave reminders like "Do I really need this?" on your wallet or phone to pause before making a purchase.

5. **Track Your Progress and Reward Yourself.** Tracking your progress helps keep you motivated. Whether it's a journal or an app, record each day you avoid the bad habit. Celebrate your small wins along the way with rewards. For instance, if you manage to go a week without falling into the habit, treat yourself to something that doesn't undermine your progress. Positive reinforcement strengthens your commitment to change.

6. **Be Patient and Persistent.** Breaking a bad habit takes time and effort, so be patient with yourself. It's normal to have setbacks but don't let them discourage you. If you slip up, acknowledge it, and refocus on your goal the next day. Each day is a new opportunity to make progress—over time, the bad habit will lose its hold on you.[8]

By following these steps, you'll be on your way to breaking the bad habit and replacing it with behaviors that bring you closer to the life you want.

How to Wield This Superpower

Here's a step-by-step process for mastering habit and routine management.

1. **Define clear objectives.** Identify what you want to achieve with your habits and routines.
2. **Assess current habits and routines.** Take inventory of your daily habits and routines to highlight areas for change.
3. **Create a structured plan.** Develop a detailed schedule that includes time for critical activities, such as school, homework, meals, exercise, hobbies, and relaxation.
4. **Integrate flexibility.** Include flexible time slots to accommodate unexpected tasks or shifts in priorities.
5. **Implement and monitor.** Put your habits and routines into practice and observe how they work in real time.
6. **Review and revise regularly.** Set regular intervals to review and adjust your habits and routines.

Training Missions to Develop This Superpower

Engage in activities such as these to enhance your habit and routine management.

- **Develop morning and evening routines.** Create and stick to routines that energize you in the morning and help you wind down in the evening.

- **Use apps to track habits.** Use habit-tracking apps to monitor your progress and boost motivation.
- **Participate in accountability groups.** Join or form groups with peers who share similar goals for support and accountability.

In the 2019 film *Avengers: Endgame,* Black Widow (Natasha Romanoff) oversees operations at Avengers HQ. She maintains a strict routine of checking in with various heroes across the universe, organizing missions, and ensuring the continuity of their efforts after the catastrophic event where Thanos wiped out half of all life in the universe. This showcases her discipline and habit of consistent leadership. Her regular check-ins with her team demonstrate how she applies routine management to keep things organized and running smoothly despite overwhelming challenges. When Natasha talks with Okoye, Rocket, Captain Marvel, and others during a holographic meeting, she is focused and systematic, ensuring the team stays on track with their individual missions. This reflects how habits and routines help her maintain order amidst chaos.

Action Items

- Before you read further, take a few minutes to consider the information presented in this section.
- Imagine yourself decades in the future (after many years of cultivating habit and routine management), and how you use this superpower to achieve your goals.
- Note how you currently employ habit and routine management in your daily life. Take pride in the progress you've already achieved in developing this superpower.
- Evaluate the effectiveness of your current practices to cultivate these skills.

- If you decide that your current efforts to cultivate habit and routine management need to be improved, consider at least one improvement you can make in the coming weeks, months, or year.
- Develop a plan for implementing that improvement.

Now that we've addressed the superpower of habit and routine management, let's move on to time management.

SUPERPOWER #22: TIME MANAGEMENT

Time management is the strategic life skill of organizing, planning, and controlling how you spend your time to achieve specific goals. It involves setting priorities, creating schedules, and making conscious decisions about how much time to dedicate to various tasks. By mastering this skill, you learn how to balance competing demands, ensuring that your focus remains on what matters most. Time management is not about doing everything but about making deliberate choices that align with your objectives and values. It requires discipline, foresight, and adaptability, allowing you to efficiently navigate short-term and long-term projects.[9]

Black Widow expertly juggles her roles as an Avenger and a spy, evidence of her time-management skills. Her ability to prioritize tasks and act quickly in high-stakes situations shows how you can make the most of your time to stay focused and productive.

The Powers of Time Management

Cultivating time management can profoundly enhance your life in several key areas. By developing this skill, you can improve your academic performance by efficiently prioritizing tasks, meeting deadlines, and eliminating the stress of last-minute cramming.

This allows you to excel in high school while still making time for personal interests and maintaining your health.

Time management also prepares you for the increased responsibility and independence required in higher education. In college, where balancing coursework, exams, and extracurricular activities is essential, a strong foundation in time management will help you succeed.[10]

As you transition to the professional world, the ability to manage your time effectively becomes even more valuable. Employers highly regard individuals who can meet deadlines, balance commitments, and operate efficiently under pressure. Proficient time management not only demonstrates your ability to handle responsibilities but also establishes a solid foundation for long-term career success. By mastering this skill, you equip yourself to thrive in any academic or professional environment.[11]

The Eisenhower Box: Prioritize Like a President

The Eisenhower Box, also known as the Eisenhower Matrix,[12] helps you prioritize tasks by urgency and importance. The matrix is divided into four quadrants.

- **Quadrant 1—Urgent and Important (Do).** Tasks requiring immediate attention that work toward long-term goals or responsibilities.
- **Quadrant 2—Important but Not Urgent (Decide).** Tasks that are important for long-term success but are not immediately pressing.
- **Quadrant 3—Urgent but Not Important (Delegate).** Tasks demanding attention but not necessarily benefiting long-term objectives.

- **Quadrant 4—Neither Urgent nor Important (Delete).** Tasks that are the least productive and can be eliminated from your schedule.[13]

Start each day or week by listing all tasks and placing them in one of the four quadrants so you can focus your efforts on what truly matters.

The 1-3-5 Method: Simplify Your Day for Maximum Productivity

Mastering time management can feel overwhelming, but the 1-3-5 method[14] offers a straightforward approach to help you stay focused and productive. This method breaks your daily tasks into manageable chunks, ensuring you tackle the most important tasks without feeling swamped. Each day, aim to complete:

- 1 Big Task
- 3 Medium Tasks
- 5 Small Tasks

Limiting the number of tasks in each category allows you to prioritize effectively and maintain a balanced workload.[15]

The Pomodoro Technique: Slicing Time to Boost Productivity

The Pomodoro Technique,[16] developed by Francesco Cirillo, is a powerful time-management method. Here's how to use it.

1. **Choose a task.** Select a task to accomplish.
2. **Set a timer.** Divide work into intervals, traditionally 25 minutes long, and set a timer accordingly.
3. **Work until the timer rings.** Dedicate yourself to the task until the timer rings.

4. **Take a short break.** Take a 5-minute break after the timer rings.
5. **Repeat.** After four intervals, take a longer break of 15-30 minutes.

Benefits include enhanced focus, increased accountability, reduced procrastination, and encouraged discipline.[17]

More Techniques for Effective Time Management

- **Prep for school the night before.** Organize your backpack, pack lunch, finish homework, and select your outfit the night before.
- **Learn to say no.** Decline requests and commitments that do not align with your priorities.
- **Have a place for everything.** Establish designated spaces for your belongings to avoid wasting time searching for items.

Following these tips can streamline your daily routines and enhance your time management skills, making your days more productive and less stressful.

Procrastination

Procrastination is the act of putting things off, even when you know there might be negative consequences.[18] There are many reasons why people procrastinate. For example, some people like the thrill of rushing around at the last minute, whereas others are worried about not being able to finish a task to perfection. Distractions can also lead to procrastination. It's a bit of a vicious circle because anxiety can lead to procrastination, but procrastination may also cause anxiety.[19]

Here are some tips for overcoming procrastination.

1. **Minimize distractions.** Identify and reduce distractions.
2. **Start with the most challenging task.** Tackle the hardest task first.
3. **Break down longer tasks.** Divide big projects into smaller tasks.
4. **Commit to a deadline.** Set and stick to realistic deadlines.
5. **Use the Two-Minute Rule.** If something can be done in less than two minutes, do it straight away.

By following these tips, you can effectively overcome procrastination and enhance your productivity.[20]

How to Wield This Superpower

Here's a step-by-step process for mastering time management.

1. **Set clear goals.** Identify what you want to achieve, whether it's completing schoolwork, preparing for an exam, or dedicating time to personal activities.
2. **Break down tasks.** Divide your goals into smaller, manageable steps, making each task easier to tackle.
3. **Prioritize your tasks.** Decide which tasks are most urgent or important and focus on those first.
4. **Create a schedule.** Use a planner, digital calendar, or app to organize your day or week. Block out specific times for each task and be realistic about how long each activity will take.
5. **Stick to your plan.** Follow the schedule as closely as possible while maintaining flexibility to adapt to changes or unexpected challenges.

6. **Review and reflect.** At the end of the day or week, assess what worked well and where you can improve. Adjust your routine to increase efficiency.

Following this process can strengthen your time management skills and develop the discipline needed to manage your responsibilities effectively.

Training Missions to Develop This Superpower

Engage in activities such as these to enhance your time management.

- **Organize your study space.** Maintaining a clean and organized study space ensures everything has a designated place. This will reduce the time spent searching for materials.
- **Take breaks and practice self-care.** Incorporate regular breaks and self-care into your schedule. Activities such as mindfulness, exercise, and hobbies can rejuvenate your mind and make you more effective during work periods.
- **Practice reflection journaling.** At the end of each day, spend a few minutes journaling about how you spent your time. Reflect on what you accomplished and where you could improve. This practice promotes continuous learning and growth in time management.
- **Use technology wisely.** Integrate apps for time management into your daily routine, but don't let them become a distraction. Turn off your notifications to reduce the temptation to pick up your phone.

Throughout the Marvel Cinematic Universe, Black Widow is known for her quick decision-making and time management, especially under pressure. In *Captain America: The Winter Soldier* (2014), Black Widow and Captain America (Steve Rogers) infiltrate S.H.I.E.L.D.'s undercover facility. Natasha efficiently divides her time between disabling security, gathering intel, and executing the mission, showing her ability to manage limited time during high-stress scenarios. When Steve and Natasha are on the run, she demonstrates how to prioritize tasks efficiently. Her quick thinking and ability to delegate what needs to be done immediately, while still focusing on long-term goals, is a great example of effective time management.

Action Items

- Before you read further, take a few minutes to consider the information presented in this section.
- Imagine yourself decades in the future (after many years of cultivating time management) and how you use this superpower to achieve your goals.
- Note how you currently employ time management in your daily life. Take pride in the progress you've already achieved in developing this superpower.
- Evaluate the effectiveness of your current practices to cultivate time management.
- If you decide that your current efforts to cultivate these skills need to be improved, consider at least one improvement you can make in the coming weeks, months, or year.
- Develop a plan for implementing that improvement.

Now that we've addressed the superpower of time management, let's move on to information management.

SUPERPOWER #23: INFORMATION MANAGEMENT

Information management is the strategic life skill of collecting, organizing, storing, and using data or knowledge in an efficient and effective manner. It involves identifying the most relevant and accurate information for a particular task or decision, as well as ensuring that the information is accessible and usable when needed. This superpower includes the ability to filter out unnecessary or irrelevant data, maintain a system for organizing information, and continually update your knowledge base to stay current. Information management requires attention to detail, a structured approach, and the ability to discern credible sources from unreliable ones, allowing you to make informed decisions.[21]

As a spy, Black Widow knows the importance of gathering and organizing information. Her success often depends on having the correct data at the right time.

The Powers of Information Management

Achieving mastery of information management can profoundly impact various aspects of your life. It enhances decision-making by helping you sort, analyze, and apply relevant data, whether you're choosing a college, planning your career, or managing personal relationships. With a clear, organized view of available information, you'll make decisions more confidently and effectively.

Proper information management also boosts productivity by preventing information overload, allowing you to quickly access resources when needed. Whether you're studying, planning a project, or solving problems, you'll be able to streamline your efforts and stay focused, avoiding unnecessary stress or procrastination.

This skill naturally sharpens your critical thinking. By evaluating the relevance and reliability of information, you'll develop a critical eye, essential for navigating academic tasks and personal situations where distinguishing fact from fiction is crucial. Additionally, managing information allows you to communicate your ideas more effectively, whether you're delivering a presentation, engaging in a debate, or having everyday conversations.

In today's digital world, information management often requires technological proficiency. By mastering the tools and platforms needed to organize data, you'll not only stay efficient but also prepare yourself for a workforce that increasingly relies on digital competence. This ability to quickly process and adapt to new information makes you more adaptable, helping you embrace new concepts and innovate solutions in a constantly changing world.

Strong information management skills are also key to developing leadership qualities. Leaders are expected to grasp the facts and articulate a vision based on accurate data. By honing this skill, you position yourself as a leader who can oversee projects, guide discussions, and make well-informed decisions.

Ultimately, mastering information management lays a solid foundation for academic excellence and career achievement, empowering you to navigate the complexities of the digital age with confidence and efficiency.

The scale of information management you need will depend on the amount and nature of the data you have. Nevertheless, there are some essentials to keep in mind.

Protecting Digital and Physical Information

Here are some tips for managing information in a digital age.

- **Use privacy settings.** Privacy settings allow you to control who can access your personal information on social media and online accounts. Regularly update these settings to ensure you're comfortable with the information being shared.
- **Be careful about sharing personal information.** Think twice before sharing personal information online. Be cautious about disclosing your full name, address, phone number, or sensitive information like your social security number.[22]
- **Be smart with passwords.** Use strong, unique passwords for your accounts. Avoid using easily guessable information like your name or birthdate. Combine letters, numbers, and symbols to create complex passwords.[23]
- **Be wary of public Wi-Fi.** Avoid accessing sensitive or personal information on public Wi-Fi networks. If necessary, use a virtual private network (VPN) to ensure a secure connection.[24]

Digital Filing Systems

Here are some tips for organizing digital information.[25]

- **Don't put files on the desktop.** Avoid cluttering your desktop screen with files. Instead, use appropriate folders to keep everything organized and easy to find.[26]
- **Limit folder creation.** Keep your folder structure simple and intuitive. Create folders based on broad categories and avoid creating unnecessary subfolders.

- **Name your files and folders strategically.** Give your files and folders clear, descriptive names to make it easier to locate specific files later.[27]

Keeping Track of Important Documents

Here are some tips for managing personal information.[28]

- **Digital and hard copies.** For extra security and accessibility, always have physical and digital copies of important documents.
- **Password protection.** You can add a password to open important documents with personal information.
- **Physical files.** Set up a physical filing system for important documents. Use an expanding file or a file box with hanging folders. Label your categories clearly.

Importance of Staying Updated

Staying updated with the latest information in your areas of interest helps you gain valuable experience, find growth opportunities, and stay ahead of others. Understanding trends can help you forecast what may happen, especially if you're looking at career opportunities. By knowing what's happening, you better understand your interests, make informed choices, and succeed in your endeavors.[29]

How to Wield This Superpower

Here's a step-by-step process for mastering information management.

1. **Define your objectives.** Understand why you need information. Clear objectives guide your search and help you stay focused.
2. **Master research.** Learn how to conduct research efficiently using search engines, evaluate sources for reliability, and synthesize information. Academic journals, government websites, and established news outlets are typically reliable sources.
3. **Organize methodically.** Organize information in a way that makes sense for your objectives. Use digital tools to categorize data.
4. **Analyze critically.** Analyze information to uncover patterns and insights. Ask critical questions to evaluate its relevance and reliability.
5. **Apply strategically.** Use information effectively to make decisions, solve problems, and present your findings clearly.
6. **Reflect and adjust.** Reflect on the process and adjust your approach as needed. Continuous improvement ensures better information management skills.

By following these steps, you can master information management, efficiently gathering, analyzing, and applying information to achieve your goals and make informed decisions.

Training Missions to Develop This Superpower

Engage in activities such as these to enhance your information management.

- **Develop digital literacy.** Become proficient in using key digital tools like word processors, spreadsheets, and presentation software.
- **Practice note-taking strategies.** Explore different note-taking methods to find what works best for you.
- **Create a personal knowledge base.** Compile a digital or physical "knowledge base" to store important information, notes, summaries, and ideas.
- **Utilize information management apps.** Learn to use project management and note-taking apps to boost your ability to organize and retrieve information quickly.
- **Set up information filters.** To manage the flow of information, use RSS feeds, email filters, and browser extensions.
- **Learn data visualization.** Understand how to represent data visually using tools like Google Charts or Tableau.
- **Review and curate content regularly.** Review your collected information regularly, delete outdated or irrelevant information, and organize existing data.

In the 2021 film *Black Widow*, Natasha Romanoff has to gather and manage a vast amount of sensitive information about the Red Room. She carefully pieces together the puzzle of who controls the Red Room and how to bring it down. She knows how to find, protect, and use information strategically, reflecting excellent information management skills. Natasha's ability to track down old information from Dreykov's daughter and use it to exploit weaknesses in the Red Room shows her mastery of gathering, analyzing, and managing critical information to achieve her goals.

Action Items

- Before you read further, take a few minutes to consider the information presented in this section.
- Imagine yourself decades in the future (after many years of cultivating information management) and how you are using this superpower to achieve your goals.
- Note how you currently employ information management in your daily life. Take pride in the progress you've already achieved in developing this superpower.
- Evaluate the effectiveness of your current practices to cultivate these skills.
- If you decide that your current efforts to cultivate information management need to be improved, consider at least one improvement you can make in the coming weeks, months, or year.
- Develop a plan for implementing that improvement.

Now that we've addressed the superpower of information management, let's move on to money management.

SUPERPOWER #24: MONEY MANAGEMENT

Money management is the strategic life skill of understanding how to effectively handle your finances—which encompasses earning, saving, budgeting, spending, and investing. It involves making intentional decisions about how to allocate your money to meet both short-term needs and long-term goals. This superpower requires you to track your income and expenses, create a budget that aligns with your priorities, and make responsible choices about saving and investing. By incorporating investments, you not only plan for your future but also seek ways to grow your wealth over time. Money management also includes preparing for unexpected expenses and making informed financial choices that support your overall financial well-being.[30]

Black Widow is resourceful, knowing how to manage limited resources under pressure. Her ability to plan and budget for missions mirrors how you can handle your finances—by saving, budgeting, and making smart investments for the future.

The Powers of Money Management

Unlocking the superpower of money management can transform multiple aspects of life. By developing this skill, you set yourself on a path toward financial independence, enabling you to make informed choices about saving, investing, and spending. With a solid understanding of how to manage your finances, you'll be able to reduce your reliance on parental support and avoid unnecessary debt, taking control of your financial future early on.[31]

Money management also fosters smart spending habits. By learning the value of budgeting, you'll become more aware of how your spending choices impact your financial stability. This skill helps you prioritize essential expenses and differentiate between needs and wants, encouraging a disciplined approach that will benefit you throughout your life.

An early introduction to investing further strengthens your financial foundation. Understanding how stocks, bonds, real estate, and other investment vehicles work puts you in a position to grow your wealth strategically, benefiting from opportunities like compound interest and market growth.

Managing your money involves mitigating risks. You'll learn to prepare for unforeseen expenses by building an emergency fund and securing yourself with the appropriate financial protections, ensuring your future is safeguarded against potential challenges. This skill becomes a crucial driver in helping you achieve personal goals, whether it's saving for college, starting a business, or purchasing your first car. By setting clear financial objectives and systematically working toward them, you can accomplish major milestones at a young age, reinforcing your confidence and perseverance.

Furthermore, managing money well enhances your understanding of how the broader economy works. Being aware of economic trends and global events helps you make informed decisions that can impact your personal finances. Ultimately, mastering money management reduces financial stress, as you'll be better equipped to handle financial uncertainty, leading to a more focused, healthy, and fulfilling life.[32]

Understanding the Value of Money

Money represents more than numbers in a bank account—it embodies your time, effort, and creativity. Each dollar is earned through physical work, mental effort, or smart investments, making it a symbol of your energy and skills. Recognizing this value encourages intentional decisions about spending, saving, and investing.[33]

Money is earned by transforming your time, knowledge, and abilities into something others value. This transformation can take different forms.

- **Physical labor** involves being paid for the hours and effort you put into tasks like lawn mowing or cashier work.

- **Mental labor** means leveraging expertise and focus, such as tutoring or coding.
- **Intellectual work** includes creating unique contributions, like books or inventions.
- **Investments** allow you to earn passively by making your money grow over time.

Each time you earn, a part of your life is exchanged, making every dollar significant.

Money, like time, is a limited resource. Each dollar spent is a choice that excludes other opportunities. Spending $20 on a movie means giving up the chance to invest or save it for a future goal. This principle, known as opportunity cost, helps guide decisions based on what matters most to you.

Your spending choices reveal what you prioritize. Saving for a musical instrument may reflect a love for learning, while donating to charity shows a value for generosity. Aligning your spending with your values ensures your money goes toward what truly matters.

Approaching money with intention doesn't mean avoiding spending—it means using it as a tool to build the life you want. By viewing each dollar as a decision point, you'll learn to spend wisely, save purposefully, and invest thoughtfully, shaping a future that aligns with your goals and values.

The Magic of Compounding

Compounding is like planting a tree—at first, growth is slow, but as the tree matures, its branches and leaves multiply, accelerating its expansion. Similarly, compounding allows your money to earn returns, which then generate returns of their own, creating a snowball effect that grows more powerful over time.[34]

How Compounding Works. Imagine investing $100 at a 10% annual return. In the first year, you earn $10, bringing your total to $110. The next year, you earn 10% on $110, making $11. By the third year, your money is growing on $121. This cycle of growth accelerates as both your initial investment and accumulated returns work together to create exponential results.

The Power of Time. Time is the key to compounding's power. The longer your money is left to grow, the more dramatic the results. For example, $100 invested at a 10% annual return grows to $259 in 10 years, $672 in 20 years, and $1,745 in 30 years. The biggest gains happen later because compounding builds momentum, making an early start crucial for maximizing growth.[35]

Beyond Money: Compounding in Life. Compounding isn't just for money—it applies to knowledge, skills, and habits. Practicing an instrument or sport daily might show little progress initially, but over time, those small efforts accumulate, leading to exponential improvement in later years. Whether it's finances or personal development, consistent effort builds on itself, turning small beginnings into substantial outcomes.

Making Compounding Work for You. To harness compounding:

1. **Start early.** The sooner you begin, the longer your efforts have to grow.
2. **Be consistent.** Regular contributions, no matter how small, add up.
3. **Be patient.** Compounding rewards those who stay the course, as its greatest benefits appear over the long term.

By using compounding, you transform small, steady inputs into extraordinary results over time. It's a system where patience and persistence pay off, turning today's small efforts into tomorrow's success.

Basic Principles of Money Management

Let's explore the basic principles of money management: budgeting, saving, and investing.[36]

- Budgeting. Think of budgeting as drafting the blueprint for your finances. Start by listing all sources of income and categorizing your expenses into essentials and nonessentials. Ensure your income exceeds your expenses, allowing room for savings and investments. Use budgeting apps or spreadsheets to visualize your financial health and make sensible decisions about spending.[37]
- Saving. Saving is the act of building a financial fortress around your future self. Set aside a portion of your income today for tomorrow's dreams or emergencies. Aim to save at least 20% of your income and consider high-interest savings accounts or certificates of deposit for higher returns. Saving focuses on preserving your wealth in safe, accessible places for short- to medium-term goals.[38] A federally insured, interest-paying bank account is a classic example.
- Investing. While saving is about safety and preservation, investing is about growth. Investing involves putting your money into assets like stocks, bonds, or real estate with the goal of increasing its value over time. Although investing carries more risk than saving, it has the potential for higher returns, helping you build wealth over the long term.[39]

Mastering money-management principles requires patience, discipline, and a willingness to learn from mistakes. And it's best to make these mistakes when the stakes are lower.

Explore Basic Investment Concepts

Venturing into the realm of investments isn't just about growing wealth—it's about embracing a mindset that values foresight, patience, and the power of compounding.

- **Investing.** Imagine if you could put your money to work instead of merely saving it, creating more wealth over time. By purchasing assets like stocks, bonds, mutual funds, or even real estate, you're planting seeds that can grow into a towering forest of financial resources.
- **Diversification.** One fundamental concept in investing is diversification. It's about spreading your investments across various assets to reduce risk. It goes back to the expression, "Don't put all your eggs in one basket."
- **Risk and return.** The relationship between risk and return is at the heart of investing. Generally, the higher the potential return, the higher the risk. Assess your risk tolerance before investing. Before investing any money, ask if you can afford to lose it.
- **Start small, think big.** Embarking on your investment journey doesn't require a fortune. Thanks to modern technology and financial innovations, you can start with small amounts.
- **Continuous education.** The world of investing is dynamic and continuously evolving. Commit to continuous education in finance and investment strategies to make informed decisions.

By embracing these concepts, you can build a strong foundation for financial growth and secure your future with patience—investing isn't a get-rich-quick scheme.

Tips on How to Avoid Common Financial Pitfalls

Being a teen means you'll probably make mistakes with your money management, and it's unlikely you'll be able to eliminate them completely as an adult. Nevertheless, there are some common mistakes you can avoid. Here are some tips to guide you.

- **Beware of impulse purchases.** Adopt a "cooling-off" period before making nonessential purchases. This pause lets you evaluate whether the purchase aligns with your goals and budget. Do you really need it?
- **Avoid high-interest debt.** If you use a credit card, aim to pay off the full balance each month to avoid interest charges. Treat credit as a tool for building a positive credit history, not an extension of your income.
- **Educate yourself in financial literacy.** Dedicate time to learning about financial basics. Numerous resources, from books and online courses to podcasts and blogs, can help you become more financially savvy.
- **Set financial goals and review them regularly.** Setting clear, achievable financial goals helps you stay focused and disciplined. Regularly review and adjust these goals as your circumstances and ambitions evolve.
- **Seek advice but consider the source.** Be wary of following financial trends or tips from social media influencers without thorough research. Advice should come from those with proven experience.

- **Be aware of financial scams.** Trust your instincts. If it sounds too good to be true, it probably is. Pressure to invest, guarantees of no risks, and not being able to answer questions are red flags.

You want to be independent, but don't let this determination lead to pitfalls. If you're in doubt, ask your parents or another trusted adult before making a financial decision.

How to Wield This Superpower

Here's a step-by-step process for mastering money management based on what we've addressed so far.

1. **Understand your financial situation.** Start by taking a clear snapshot of your current financial situation. List your sources of income and note all your expenses.
2. **Set clear financial goals.** Define what you want to achieve with your money. Be specific about how much you want to save and by when.
3. **Create a budget.** Allocate your income to different categories, such as savings, essentials, and discretionary spending.
4. **Save and invest wisely.** It's never too early to start saving and reduce the risk of financial stress in the future. Consider putting a portion of your savings into higher-interest accounts or investments.
5. **Track your spending.** Monitor your spending habits closely. Use a money management app or a simple spreadsheet to track your expenses.
6. **Develop financial literacy.** Educate yourself regarding basic financial concepts like interest rates, credit scores, and investment options.

7. **Practice self-discipline.** Avoid impulse purchases and ensure that your spending aligns with your financial goals.

8. **Seek the right guidance.** Talk to a trusted adult or financial advisor about your plans and decisions.[40]

Training Missions to Develop This Superpower

Engage in activities such as these to enhance your money-management skills.

- **Open a bank account.** Research different accounts, paying attention to any fees. Manage your account, understanding responsibilities like monitoring balances and saving regularly.
- **Participate in savings challenges.** To teach discipline, save a certain amount each week or cut out unnecessary expenses.
- **Hold a family financial meeting.** Gain perspective on household finances, bills, and financial decision-making.
- **Learn through games.** Financial literacy games can engage players in learning about money management. They could be traditional board games or games from app stores.[41]
- **Earn and manage money.** Part-time jobs or freelance gigs teach the value of work and managing earnings.
- **Simulate stock market investments.** Engage in simulations to understand market dynamics and the impact of economic changes.[42]
- **Give to charities.** Set aside a portion of money for charity to foster empathy and responsibility.

Though money management is not overtly portrayed, Natasha Romanoff's ability to live off the grid and resourcefully manage her finances can be inferred throughout *Black Widow* (2021). She operates without the support of government resources or S.H.I.E.L.D. funding after being declared a fugitive. Her ability to travel, secure supplies, and maintain her lifestyle speaks to her savvy financial management. Natasha's nomadic life in Black Widow suggests that she has the means to live frugally yet efficiently. She stays off the radar, purchasing essentials without drawing attention to herself, which speaks to practical money management—spending wisely, planning ahead, and managing assets effectively.

Action Items

- Before you read further, take a few minutes to consider the information presented in this section.
- Imagine yourself decades in the future (after many years of cultivating money-management skills) and how you use this superpower to achieve your goals.
- Note how you currently employ money management in your daily life. Take pride in the progress you've already achieved in developing this superpower.
- Evaluate the effectiveness of your current practices to cultivate these skills.
- If you decide that your current efforts to cultivate money-management skills need to be improved, consider at least one improvement you can make in the coming weeks, months, or year.
- Develop a plan for implementing that improvement.

Now that we've addressed the superpower of money management, let's move on to career management.

SUPERPOWER #25: CAREER MANAGEMENT

Career management is the strategic life skill of actively planning and directing your professional journey. It involves setting career goals, developing the skills and qualifications needed to achieve those goals, and making informed decisions about education, job opportunities, and career growth. This superpower requires ongoing self-assessment, adaptability, and a focus on building a strong professional network. Career management also encompasses navigating workplace dynamics, seeking out mentorship, and continually refining your personal brand. It's about taking ownership of your career trajectory and being proactive in shaping your professional future.[43]

Black Widow's career showcases adaptability and strategic growth. From a spy to an Avenger, she's always refining her skills and navigating new challenges. Like her, you can manage your career by setting clear goals, learning new skills, and staying adaptable.

The Powers of Career Management

Developing the superpower of career management can lead to improvements in many areas of your life. By developing clarity and direction, you define what success means to you and set clear goals to guide your journey. This creates a roadmap for your education, job opportunities, and professional development, giving you a solid foundation for making informed choices.[44]

Career management also enhances your decision-making skills, enabling you to critically assess opportunities and challenges. Each decision becomes a stepping stone that moves you closer to your desired career path. As you navigate this path, you'll develop adaptability and resilience, equipping yourself to handle unexpected shifts in the job market or personal circumstances. This flexibility allows you to pivot when needed and continue thriving despite setbacks.

With a well-managed career, your confidence will naturally grow. Knowing where you're headed and having a plan to get there boosts your self-assurance, making you more poised during job interviews, networking events,[45] and other professional interactions. You also commit to continuous growth and learning, ensuring that you stay current with industry trends and consistently improve your skills, which keeps you competitive and valuable in your chosen field.

By aligning your work with your passions and strengths, career management increases your likelihood of finding greater job satisfaction. You'll also position yourself for better job opportunities and higher earning potential, providing financial stability that enhances your overall quality of life. Furthermore, as you actively manage your career, you'll build a strong professional network that offers mentorship, advice, and potential career opportunities.

Mastering career management allows you to pursue a fulfilling, successful career with confidence and strategic intent.

How to Wield This Superpower

Here's a step-by-step process for mastering career management.

1. **Self-assessment.** Understand your strengths, weaknesses, interests, and values. Tools like personality tests or career assessments can be useful.
2. **Goal setting.** Set SMART career goals. Think about where you want to be in five, ten, or twenty years. Break the goals into smaller steps and focus on your short-term planning and how you can integrate this into your current studies.[46]

3. **Skill acquisition.** Identify the skills and education necessary to achieve your career goals. Choose relevant courses, seek out internships, or engage in self-directed learning, such as free online courses.
4. **Networking.** Attend workshops, seminars, and networking events to connect with mentors, teachers, and professionals in your desired industry.[47]
5. **Experience gathering.** Participate in internships, volunteer work, or part-time jobs[48] in your chosen field. Each experience builds skills, enhances your resume, and provides clearer career insights.
6. **Adaptability.** Stay flexible and be willing to adapt your goals and strategies based on industry trends and personal interests.
7. **Reflection and Reassessment.** Regularly evaluate your career path. Make it a habit to reassess your goals and strategies annually or during a significant change.
8. **Persistence and resilience** Managing your career is a marathon, not a sprint. Pursue your goals with persistence, developing resilience in the face of setbacks.

A word of caution—be wary of the portrayal of careers on television and in the movies. We see software engineers coding in seconds, lawyers making powerful and intimidating speeches, and law enforcement officers constantly engaged in adrenaline rushes. These shows are intended to be dramatic, but they might attract you to a career that is very different in real life.

Training Missions to Develop This Superpower

Engage in activities such as these to enhance your career management.

- **Be proactive.** Actively explore different career paths. Contact professionals in fields that interest you for informational interviews or shadowing opportunities.
- **Do your research.** Investigate different careers by conducting online research, reading books, or attending career fairs.
- **Speak with a career counselor.** Talk to a career counselor to help identify your interests, strengths, and values.
- **Use job search assistance.** When ready to start searching for a job or internship, utilize resources such as job boards, career centers, and networking events.
- **Take on challenges.** Step out of your comfort zone and take on new challenges to gain valuable experience.
- **Acquire transferable skills.** Focus on building communication, teamwork, problem-solving, time management, and leadership skills, as they'll be beneficial for various careers.

Natasha Romanoff's journey in the Marvel Cinematic Universe is an excellent example of career management, from her time as a Russian spy to becoming an Avenger. In *Black Widow* (2021), Natasha confronts her past while managing her present identity as a hero. She makes strategic career decisions, transitioning from a S.H.I.E.L.D. agent to a superhero, and even takes control of her narrative by breaking away from her former controllers. For example, when Natasha decides to face the Red Room in *Black Widow*, she demonstrates her ability to manage her career trajectory, balancing her past and future. By severing ties with toxic influences and taking control of her legacy, she models how to take charge of one's career development and growth.

Action Items

- Before you read further, take a few minutes to consider the information presented in this section.
- Imagine yourself decades in the future (after many years of cultivating career-management skills), and how you're using this superpower to achieve your goals.
- Note how you currently employ career management in your daily life. Take pride in the progress you've already achieved in developing this superpower.
- Evaluate the effectiveness of your current practices to cultivate these skills.
- If you decide that your current career-management efforts need to be improved, consider at least one improvement you can make in the coming weeks, months, or year.
- Develop a plan for implementing that improvement.

Having equipped yourself with the tools for practical life management, you can now look to shaping your technology and learning skills. In the next chapter, we'll explore how embracing numeracy, technology skills, and learning skills can further empower you to become a real-life superhero.

TECHNOLOGY AND LEARNING SKILLS

In today's fast-paced world, mastering the ability to learn is one of the most valuable skills you can develop. Learning isn't just about absorbing information—it's about understanding how to approach new challenges and adapt to a constantly changing environment. This chapter focuses on three key life skills that form the foundation of effective learning: numeracy, technology skills, and learning skills.

We can draw inspiration from Cyborg, a superhero whose essence combines advanced technology and human intellect, reflecting the importance of being technologically savvy and adaptable today.[1]

Given that many technological applications and tools require a fundamental grasp of numerical concepts, our journey begins with numeracy.

SUPERPOWER #26: NUMERACY

Numeracy is the ability to understand and work with numbers, applying mathematical concepts and reasoning to everyday situations. It involves performing calculations, interpreting data, recognizing patterns, and solving quantitative problems. This skill encompasses not only basic arithmetic but also a deeper comprehension of how numbers relate to each other, whether in finance, measurements, or statistics. Numeracy allows individuals to make informed decisions, analyze information, and approach challenges with a logical and methodical mindset.[2]

Cyborg's analytical abilities highlight the importance of numeracy in today's data-driven world. His mastery of complex calculations and pattern recognition allows him to process vast amounts of data in seconds.

The Powers of Numeracy

Harnessing the power of numeracy can enhance your life in many ways. With a solid grasp of numbers, you'll develop financial savvy, enabling you to create and manage a budget, track your spending, and save toward future goals. You'll also be able to compare interest rates, understand loan terms, and steer clear of debt traps, laying the groundwork for financial security.

In school and in your career, strong numeracy skills give you a competitive edge. They boost your performance across various subjects, not just in math, and can open doors to scholarships, advanced courses, and special recognition. Many high-demand careers—such as those in engineering, technology, finance, and health sciences—require a deep understanding of numbers.

Numeracy also sharpens your critical thinking and problem-solving skills, allowing you to break down complex situations, analyze data, and arrive at sound conclusions. Whether in academic settings or everyday life, this ability will guide you toward more effective solutions. Additionally, numeracy empowers you to make informed decisions. You'll be able to assess options, consider probabilities, and choose based on reason rather than impulse, increasing your chances of achieving your goals.

With numeracy, you'll gain confidence and independence. Understanding numbers ensures you're not intimidated by financial jargon, complex data, or challenging problems.[3] Instead, you'll approach these situations with confidence, knowing you have the skills to handle them effectively.

How to Wield This Superpower

Here's a step-by-step process for mastering numeracy.

1. **Fundamental understanding.** Start with a solid foundation in basic arithmetic—addition, subtraction, multiplication, and division. Ensure you understand fractions, decimals, and percentages.[4]
2. **Critical thinking.** Use numeracy as a tool for critical thinking. Question numbers and statistics presented to you, engaging with them analytically.
3. **Problem solving.** Incorporate numeracy into your problem-solving toolkit by breaking problems into numerical components for analysis.
4. **Statistical reasoning.** Develop an understanding of probability and statistics to interpret data correctly and make informed predictions.

5. **Technology integration.** Leverage technology to enhance your numeracy skills using apps and software for calculations and data analysis.

6. **Communication.** Learn to communicate your numerical findings effectively through graphs, reports, and presentations, ensuring others understand and act on your analysis.

By mastering these steps, you can enhance your numeracy skills, which will empower you to tackle real-life problems, make informed decisions, and effectively communicate your findings.

Training Missions to Develop This Superpower

Engage in activities such as these to enhance your numeracy.

- **Practice estimating.** Practice estimating quantities, distances, and costs in your daily life.
- **Learn geometry.** Explore geometric concepts by identifying shapes, measuring angles, and understanding geometric properties.
- **Improve financial skills.** Learn about budgeting, saving, and investing to strengthen your numeracy and financial literacy.
- **Interpret graphs and charts.** Develop the ability to create, interpret, and analyze different types of graphs and recognize trends and patterns.
- **Scrutinize news and media.** Practice evaluating data sources, understanding sample sizes, and identifying biases in presented data.
- **Play math games.** Engage in fun math games and activities to make learning numeracy more enjoyable and to practice foundational math skills and problem-solving.[5]

In the 2021 film *Zack Snyder's Justice League*, Cyborg (Victor Stone) exemplifies advanced numeracy skills through his ability to manipulate global financial systems. One standout scene demonstrates his mastery when he accesses and reconfigures complex financial data streams to assist a struggling woman, depositing a substantial sum of money into her bank account. This moment highlights his technical prowess and underscores how numeracy extends beyond mere calculations—it involves interpreting data and recognizing patterns that can profoundly impact people's lives.[6]

Action Items

- Before you read further, take a few minutes to consider the information presented in this section.
- Imagine yourself decades in the future (after many years of cultivating numeracy), and how you're using this superpower to achieve your goals.
- Note how you currently employ numeracy in your daily life. Take pride in the progress you've already achieved in developing this superpower.
- Evaluate the effectiveness of your current practices to cultivate these skills.
- If you decide that your current efforts to cultivate numeracy need to be improved, consider at least one improvement you can make in the coming weeks, months, or year.
- Develop a plan for implementing that improvement.

Now that we've addressed the superpower of numeracy, let's move on to technology skills.

SUPERPOWER #27: TECHNOLOGY SKILLS

Technology skills refer to the ability to effectively use and interact with digital tools, software, and devices. These skills encompass a wide range of competencies, including understanding how to navigate computer systems, use various applications, and work with devices like smartphones, tablets, and computers. Technology skills also involve knowing how to troubleshoot common issues, manage online platforms, and stay updated with emerging technologies. They include both basic functions, such as using word processors and communication tools, and more advanced tasks like coding, data analysis, and working with specialized software or hardware. Mastery of these skills allows individuals to adapt to a rapidly changing digital landscape, ensuring they can operate efficiently and confidently in various environments.[7]

Cyborg's integration of technology into his very being illustrates the power of tech skills in modern life. His ability to seamlessly interact with digital systems, solve technical problems, and adapt to new software and hardware demonstrates how crucial it is to stay current with evolving technology. By mastering tech skills, you, too, can navigate the digital landscape like Cyborg, using technology as a tool to enhance your capabilities and solve challenges creatively.

The Powers of Technology Skills

Mastering technology skills can significantly enhance your life in multiple ways. It increases your learning capacity and adaptability, enabling you to tackle new challenges with confidence. From navigating new software to accessing information online, your ability to learn and process information becomes more efficient. Technology also improves your problem-solving abilities, providing you with tools like spreadsheets, algorithms, and simulations to analyze data and tackle complex issues through logical reasoning.

Your creativity is greatly expanded through digital tools like graphic design programs, video editing software, and digital music platforms. These tools allow you to create visually captivating presentations, engaging multimedia content, and original art, setting you apart in various fields. In terms of career, technology plays a vital role across industries, and having strong tech skills early on opens the door to a wide array of career opportunities, making you a versatile and desirable candidate in the workforce.

Technology also enhances communication, allowing you to connect through emails, instant messages, and collaborative platforms. By mastering these tools, you can effectively reach broader audiences and communicate more clearly. Beyond communication, technology skills improve your ability to network and collaborate with people globally, using tools like online forums, social media, and collaboration platforms.

Lastly, technology helps streamline your personal management. Tools for time management, project tracking, and financial planning enable you to stay organized and efficiently manage your responsibilities. Developing strong technology skills equips you to thrive in an increasingly digital world.[8]

How to Wield This Superpower

Here's a step-by-step process for mastering technology skills.

1. **Mastering the fundamentals.** Expand your technological toolkit by mastering essential software like word processors, spreadsheets, and presentation software. Dive

into graphic design with tools like Canva and Adobe
Photoshop or video editing with software like Final
Cut Pro.

2. **Staying safe online.** Protect your personal information by
   using strong, unique passwords, being cautious while
   sharing private details, and familiarizing yourself with
   privacy settings on social media platforms. When shopping
   online, only use secure payment methods and watch out
   for scams and phishing (emails that look like legitimate
   companies but are just scams).[9]

3. **Creating and editing your work.** Develop skills in
   creating, editing, and formatting online documents using
   platforms like Google Docs or Microsoft Office 365.
   Practice with free software to edit photos, videos, and
   music, which can help with web design, social media
   campaigns, and marketing in the future.

4. **Get coding.** Explore the basics of computer science, such
   as coding and programming. Engage with platforms like
   Codecademy or Scratch to learn coding through
   interactive projects and challenges.

5. **Familiarize yourself with artificial intelligence.** It's
   estimated that by 2025, AI will have created over 90
   million jobs. A core role of AI is automation, which is
   streamlining processes in the workplace across a wide
   range of industries.[10]

6. **Be responsible.** Understand the etiquette of online
   communication.[11] Be respectful and mindful of others and
   use your technological prowess to contribute positively to
   society.

By following these steps, you can master technology skills, enabling you to navigate the digital world confidently and responsibly while leveraging technology to enhance your personal and professional life.

Training Missions to Develop This Superpower

Engage in activities such as these to enhance your technology skills.

- **Join tech clubs or competitions.** Look for clubs in your school or community that focus on technology, such as a robotics club or a coding team. Participating in competitions like hackathons can also help you develop your skills further.
- **Create digital content.** Start a blog, a YouTube channel, or a podcast to gain practical experience. This will develop your technical skills in managing digital platforms and enhance your content creation abilities.
- **Develop problem-solving skills with tech tools.** Use technology to solve everyday problems. Learn to utilize tools like spreadsheets for budgeting or project management software to organize school projects.
- **Stay updated on tech trends.** Follow relevant blogs, podcasts, and news sites to stay informed about the latest in tech. Understanding emerging technologies like artificial intelligence, blockchain, or virtual reality could inspire your next big project.
- **Experiment with hardware.** Start small with DIY kits for building computers or basic electronics. Platforms like Raspberry Pi or Arduino provide a hands-on approach to learning how hardware and software interact.

- **Volunteer for tech-based projects.** Many nonprofits and local businesses need tech support. Volunteering your time to help with their website or data management builds your skills, enhances your resume, and provides valuable networking opportunities.

In the 2021 film *Zack Snyder's Justice League*, Cyborg (Victor Stone) showcases his exceptional technology skills throughout the story. His cybernetic enhancements grant him the ability to interface seamlessly with any digital system. Notably, he hacks into alien technology, decoding the workings of the Mother Boxes and devising a plan to prevent their unification. His effortless command of both terrestrial and extraterrestrial systems underscores his mastery of digital and physical technology. This illustrates that true technological expertise goes beyond merely using tools—it's about innovating new applications and solutions in critical, high-stakes situations.[12]

Action Items

- Before you read further, take a few minutes to consider the information presented in this section.
- Imagine yourself decades in the future (after many years of cultivating technology skills), and how you're using this superpower to achieve your goals.
- Note how you currently employ technology skills in your daily life. Take pride in the progress you've already achieved in developing this superpower.
- Evaluate the effectiveness of your current practices to cultivate these skills.
- If you decide that your current efforts to cultivate technology skills need to be improved, consider at least one improvement you can make in the coming weeks,

months, or year.
- Develop a plan for implementing that improvement.

Now that we've addressed the superpower of technology skills, let's move on to learning skills.

SUPERPOWER #28: LEARNING SKILLS

Learning skills refer to the ability to effectively acquire, process, and retain new information, allowing individuals to adapt to changing environments and challenges. These skills include techniques for understanding and remembering material, such as note-taking, summarizing, and applying knowledge in different contexts. Learning skills also encompass critical aspects like curiosity, self-discipline, and the ability to stay focused and organized when tackling new subjects. They involve developing strategies for problem-solving, understanding complex concepts, and applying different learning methods, such as visual, auditory, or kinesthetic techniques, to suit various needs.[13]

Cyborg's constant upgrades and adaptability exemplify the superpower of learning skills. His ability to continually evolve by integrating new technologies reflects the importance of lifelong learning. Like Cyborg, you can stay ahead of the curve by developing effective learning strategies, constantly improving your abilities, and staying curious about the world around you.

The Powers of Learning Skills

Strengthening your learning skills can greatly enhance your life by enabling you to navigate an ever-changing world. The ability to continually learn and adapt keeps you informed about technological advancements, emerging trends, and industry shifts, making you versatile and well-prepared for whatever the future holds. Lifelong learning also ensures that your career stays relevant, as it refreshes and expands your skill set, positioning you as an essential contributor within any team or organization.

On a personal level, lifelong learning encourages you to explore new subjects, consider diverse perspectives, and push the boundaries of your understanding. This intellectual curiosity fosters growth and a deeper connection to the world around you. Additionally, cultivating learning skills helps you develop resilience and flexibility, empowering you to bounce back from setbacks and handle change with greater ease.

Engaging in continuous learning also provides a sense of purpose and achievement. Every new skill you master or concept you grasp brings a sense of accomplishment that enriches your life, offering both personal fulfillment and joy. By honing your learning skills, you equip yourself not only for academic and career success but also for a lifetime of personal evolution and growth.[14]

How to Wield This Superpower

Here's a step-by-step process for mastering learning skills.

1. **Embrace a growth mindset.** Recognize that your capabilities can be enhanced through effort and perseverance, nurturing a passion for learning and resilience.[15]
2. **Set clear goals.** Establish specific, time-bound goals to keep your learning directed and purposeful, such as being able to speak a new language within three months.[16]
3. **Choose the right resources.** Select materials that match your learning style, such as textbooks, online courses, tutorials, podcasts, or interactive apps.

4. **Create a dedicated study schedule.** Develop good study habits[17] and allocate specific times for focused study sessions to build a routine and manage your time efficiently.[18]

5. **Practice active learning.** Engage with the material by taking notes,[19] summarizing, teaching it to others, or applying it in practical projects for deeper understanding and long-term retention.

6. **Test yourself Regularly.** Use quizzes, flashcards, and practice tests to reinforce your knowledge and identify areas needing more attention.

7. **Embrace mistakes as learning opportunities.** View mistakes as opportunities to learn and adjust your approach.[20]

8. **Seek feedback.** Ask teachers, mentors, or peers for feedback to refine your learning methods.

9. **Stay flexible.** Remain open to new methods and adjust your strategies for more effective learning outcomes.

By following these steps, you can master learning skills, enabling you to approach new challenges confidently, adapt to various learning environments, and continuously grow your knowledge and abilities.

Training Missions to Develop This Superpower

Engage in activities such as these to enhance your learning skills.

- **Practice mind mapping.** Visualize information with mind maps to structure thoughts and connect ideas.
- **Teach others.** Organize study groups to teach concepts to your peers, solidifying your knowledge and identifying areas needing clarification.

- **Take online courses.** Explore free and paid courses on platforms like Coursera, edX, or Udemy, which often include forums for discussing concepts with learners worldwide.
- **Use educational apps.** Use apps like Duolingo or Khan Academy to improve critical thinking, problem-solving, and communication skills.
- **Keep a learning journal.** Reflect on your learning by writing down what you learned, your questions, and how to apply the knowledge.

In the 2021 film *Zack Snyder's Justice League*, Cyborg (Victor Stone) is in a constant state of learning and adaptation as he navigates his newly acquired abilities, including the power to interface with technology on a global scale. As he evolves into his new form, Cyborg embarks on a journey of self-discovery, learning to control his advanced technological interfaces and powers while deepening his understanding of his connection to the world's digital networks. His learning process exemplifies self-directed, adaptive, and resilient skills. Rather than merely accepting his new capabilities, Cyborg actively learns to harness them in increasingly creative ways, ultimately contributing to the team's success.[21]

Action Items

- Before you read further, take a few minutes to consider the information presented in this section.
- Imagine yourself decades in the future (after many years of cultivating learning skills) and how you're using this superpower to achieve your goals.
- Note how you currently employ learning skills in your daily life. Take pride in the progress you've already achieved in developing this superpower.

- Evaluate the effectiveness of your current practices to cultivate these skills.
- If you decide that your current efforts to cultivate learning skills need to be improved, consider at least one improvement you can make in the coming weeks, months, or year.
- Develop a plan for implementing that improvement.

Think again of Cyborg, who seamlessly blends cutting-edge technology with human intuition and intellect to overcome challenges. Technology and learning skills prepare you to meet the demands of the modern world where you plan to excel. Cyborg's ability to adapt his technological components for various scenarios mirrors the flexibility and innovative thinking required of tomorrow's leaders. Embracing these superpowers enables you to not only navigate but also shape the future, leveraging technology as a tool for unprecedented achievements. As we close this chapter, remember that, like Cyborg, you can harness technology to extend your capabilities, solve complex problems, and transform obstacles into opportunities.[22]

Shout Your Superpowers Out from the Rooftops

You now have 28 superpowers under your belt, and I'm going to ask you once again to use that extra power to help other teens. When you let others know they can also embrace these life skills, they can transform their lives just like you. It's not just about making sure you all enjoy your teen years—it's about a future where you thrive together, positively impacting the world. Reviews make that possible.

YOUR OPINION MATTERS!
LEAVE A REVIEW TO HELP
OTHERS JUST LIKE YOU

You might not think your words are enough to make a difference, but to a struggling teen, they could be exactly what they need to hear. I promise it only takes a couple of minutes and a few clicks, and I will be so grateful. On top of that, I get to hear about your superhero adventures.

>>> **Click here to leave your review on Amazon.**

In the conclusion of this book, we'll bring everything together to help you plan your next steps.

CONCLUSION

Throughout this journey, we've explored life's challenges and the superpowers needed to overcome them. From managing emotions and forging strong relationships to conquering the digital world and beyond, you've gained a comprehensive set of skills tailored to enduring life's trials and flourishing amid them. These skills collectively forge the path to becoming a well-rounded, empowered individual ready to take on the world.

The path of a hero is not marked by the absence of adversity but by the courage to face it head-on. The skills and insights shared within these pages are your allies, guiding lights in moments of darkness and uncertainty. But the true transformation lies within you—the choices you make, the challenges you embrace, and the perseverance you exhibit.

The journey of self-discovery and mastery is ongoing, and each day presents new opportunities for growth, learning, and self-improvement. The world around you is ever-changing, and with the skills you've acquired, you're prepared to adapt and evolve.

Next Steps

As I mentioned at the beginning, this book includes a lot of information—way too much to implement within a short timeframe. Remember what Desmond Tutu said about how to eat an elephant —one bite at a time.[1] That's good advice, but it doesn't answer the question of "Where do I start?" The answer to that question will vary from individual to individual, but the following paragraphs provide guidance.

Progress Already Made

Take heart in acknowledging what you've already accomplished. At the end of each superpower section in this book, there's a list of action steps reflecting on not just where you need to improve but what you're already doing. You may not have considered the skills and knowledge you've gained as superpowers—but now you realize how valuable they are. Congratulations on your progress to date!

Also, take a moment to be thankful for your parents, teachers, coaches, and anyone else who has guided you along the way so far. They, too, probably didn't think about superpowers, but they knew you'd need certain knowledge and skills, and they, no doubt, encouraged, helped, and probably pushed you along the way. Just as young Luke Skywalker of Star Wars unwittingly honed the dormant Force within him while shooting womp rats on planet Tatooine, you've been developing superpowers all your life.

You're Already Doing It!

Not only have you already made substantial progress in developing your superpowers, but you also continue to do so. Most likely, as a teenager, you're enrolled in school, being home-schooled, or participating in some other organized educational program. If so, most of your waking hours are already devoted to acquiring knowledge and skills, even if you haven't considered them superpowers. So, what's the easiest way to grow your super-powers faster and stronger? Embrace the education you're already receiving with renewed vigor and enthusiasm. Be a real-life Spider-Man—outwardly a student, secretly a superhero! Dig into homework with gusto, view tests and quizzes as welcome chal-lenges, and relish special projects as opportunities to hone your powers. Likewise, view your extracurricular activities and home life as superpower-growing experiences.

Low-Hanging Fruit

As you were reading this book, I suspect you noted some changes in your behavior that you can easily implement. For example, while reading about stress management, you might have decided that whenever you feel growing anxiety, you'll take slow and deep breaths. Regarding wellness management, you might add drinking one glass of water to your morning routine. For self-reflection, you might develop the habit of quiet mindfulness for a few minutes before bedtime. Do these ideas seem insignificant? Remember the power of compounding—over time, even tiny increments of change can create huge benefits. Harvest low-hanging fruit to grow your superpowers.

Habit of Habits

You can cultivate your superpowers by managing your portfolio of habits. Nourish good habits and prune bad ones. Often, a habit can take some weeks to become solidly engrained. Once you're satisfied that these behaviors are part of your life, find new improvements to develop. If you repeat this process throughout your life, you'll continue to grow your superpowers, getting closer and closer to the superhero you want to become.

Short-Term Goals

As you progressed through this book and addressed the action steps after each superpower, you identified various improvements to achieve during the coming weeks, months, and year. For each of those, you developed a plan for its achievement. To avoid overburdening yourself and adding unnecessary stress, establish a doable timeline for completing your action steps. Look for ways to make your action steps fun—the superpower journey can be entertaining, satisfying, and rewarding. Remember the superpower of personal responsibility—you're in charge of your life.

Long-Term Goals

If you haven't already done so, write a personal vision statement and revisit the section about strategic thinking. Consistent with your vision statement, imagine what you would like to be doing in ten or twenty years, and then develop a plan to make that vision a reality.

An Ending and a Beginning

As you move forward, remember that the superpowers addressed in this book are not just lessons to be learned—they're principles to live by. Your journey through adolescence into adulthood will be filled with moments of triumph and trials, but equipped with your superpowers, you're ready to face them with confidence and grace.

This book may have concluded, but your adventure is just beginning. The skills you've learned are the seeds of your future success, ready to be nurtured and grown. Life will test your resolve, patience, and commitment, but remember—you're the hero of your own story. Each challenge is an opportunity to demonstrate your superpowers, to rise above, and to fulfill your ambitions.

Keep exploring, learning, and growing as you continue on your path. The world is vast, filled with mysteries to uncover and challenges to conquer. With the foundation you've built, there's no limit to what you can achieve.

In the spirit of the heroes who have inspired us, you, too, can be an inspiration for others. Imagine joining the workforce with colleagues who are emotionally intelligent problem solvers, where together, you can combine your ideas and uniqueness to make impactful changes the world desperately needs. For this to happen, more teens need access to information to help them develop life skills and their superpowers. By posting a short review of this book on Amazon, you can let other teens know that they, too, can thrive through the challenges ahead of them. Your voice matters!

Thank you for allowing me to be a part of your journey. This ending is just the beginning. Let's turn the page together and enter a future where you're a real-life superhero ready to impact the world.

EXPLORE OTHER WORKS BY MIKE KLAASSEN

NONFICTION

How to Write a Novel That Matters: Crafting Stories with the Power to Captivate, Enlighten, and Inspire

Third-Person Possessed: How to Write Page-Turning Fiction for 21st Century Readers

Scenes and Sequels: How to Write Page-Turning Fiction

Fiction-Writing Modes: Eleven Essential Tools for Bringing Your Story to Life

HISTORICAL FICTION

Backlash: A War of 1812 Novel

YOUNG-ADULT NOVELS

Cracks

The Brute

KLAASSEN'S CLASSIC FOLKTALES

Jack and the Beanstalk: The Old English Story Told as a Novella

Cinderella: The Brothers Grimm Story Told as a Novella

The Frog Prince: The Brothers Grimm Story Told as a Novella

Hansel and Gretel: The Brothers Grimm Story Told as a Novella

ABOUT THE AUTHOR

Mike Klaassen writes thought-provoking and action-filled narratives about young protagonists confronting significant challenges. His works, including *The Brute, Cracks,* and *Backlash: A War of 1812 Novel,* display dynamic storytelling and compelling character development.

Driven by a passion for continuous learning and research, Mike delved into the art of storytelling, producing a series of insightful books about the craft of writing fiction. These books offer practical guidance for aspiring writers and illuminate the processes behind compelling storytelling.

Fusing his love for folklore with his skill in fiction, Mike initiated "Klaassen's Classic Folktales," a collection that retells ancient stories as novellas. Through this series, he breathes new life into time-honored tales, offering readers of all ages a fresh perspective on these enduring stories.

As a proud father and grandfather, Mike believes that each generation encounters unique opportunities and challenges, which inspired him to write *Superpower Life Skills for Teens with Ambition.*

INDEX

BIBLIOGRAPHY

BACKGROUND

Brennan, Dan, MD. "Teenagers: Why do they rebel?" MedicineNet. Accessed May 10, 2024. https://www.webmd.com/parenting/features/teenagers-why-do-they-rebel#.

Divecha, Diana. "How Teens Today Are Different from Past Generations." Greater Good Magazine. University of California Berkeley. October 20, 2017. https://greatergood.berkeley.edu/article/item/how_teens_today_are_different_from_past_generations.

Mental Health America. "Youth Ranking 2023." Accessed May 10, 2024. https://www.mhanational.org/issues/2023/mental-health-america-youth-data.

Momentous Institute. "Mental Health in 2023: Teens." June 14, 2023. https://momentousinstitute.org/resources/mental-health-in-2023-teens.

My Strengths. "The Emerging Issues Facing Teens in 2023 (and how educators can help)." Greater Good Science Center. Parenting and Family. January 17, 2023. https://hub.mystrengths.com.au/user-guides/the-emerging-issues-facing-teens-in-2023-and-how-educators-can-help/.

Vogels, Emily A., and Gelles-Watnick, Risa. "Teens and Social Media: Key findings from Pew Research Center surveys." Pew Research Center. April 24, 2023. https://www.pewresearch.org/short-reads/2023/04/24/teens-and-social-media-key-findings-from-pew-research-center-surveys/.

AMBITION

BetterHelp. "What Does Ambition Mean? Learn About the Pursuit of Achievement." Updated August 13, 2024. https://www.betterhelp.com/advice/ambition/what-does-ambition-mean-an-overview/.

CIO Views. "What Does It Mean to Have Ambition." Accessed September 20, 2024. https://cioviews.com/what-does-it-mean-to-have-ambition/.

Perry, Elizabeth. "12 Ambition Examples That'll Inspire Your Goal-Setting." BetterUp. October 9, 2023. https://www.betterup.com/blog/examples-of-ambition.

INTRODUCTION

Akkas, Farzana. "Youth Suicide Risk Increased Over Past Decade." The Pew Charitable Trusts. March 3, 2023. https://www.pewtrusts.org/en/research-and-analysis/articles/2023/03/03/youth-suicide-risk-increased-over-past-decade.

Anti-Bullying Alliance. "Prevalence of Online Bullying." Accessed September 17, 2024. https://anti-bullyingalliance.org.uk/tools-information/all-about-bully ing/prevalence-and-impact-bullying/prevalence-online-bullying.

A-Z Quotes. "Desmond Tutu Quote." Accessed September 17, 2024. https://www. azquotes.com/quote/529521.

Davis, Tchika, MA, PhD. "Life Skills: Definition, Examples, & Skills to Build." Berkeley Well-Being Institute. Accessed May 10, 2024. https://www.berkeley wellbeing.com/life-skills.html.

Future Learn. "Neuroplasticity and Memory." Accessed September 17, 2024. https://www.futurelearn.com/info/courses/learning-and-memory/0/steps/ 112023.

Mental Health America. "Youth Ranking 2023." Accessed May 10, 2024. https:// www.mhanational.org/issues/2023/mental-health-america-youth-data.

SkillsYouNeed. "Life Skills." Accessed May 10, 2024. https://www.skillsyouneed. com/general/life-skills.html.

United Nations. "Eight Trends That Will Impact Children in 2023." UN News. Global perspective human stories: Culture and Education. January 31, 2023. https://news.un.org/en/story/2023/01/1132937.

CHAPTER 1: HOLISTIC WELL-BEING

Celebz Post. "Lessons from Batman: The five keys to self-improvement mastery." March 5, 2023. https://www.celebzpost.com/2023/03/five-keys-to-self-improvement-from-batman.html?m=1.

Mallory Holland, Taylor. "Dignity Health | What Is Holistic Health Care, Anyway?" Dignity Health. January 24, 2018. https://www.dignityhealth.org/articles/ what-is-holistic-health-care-anyway#:

Martin, Tina. "Holistic Approaches to Well-Being and Health." Creative Healthcare Management. January 18, 2024. https://chcm.com/holistic-approaches-to-well-being-and-health/.

SUPERPOWER #1: STRESS MANAGEMENT

Beresin, Gene, MD, MA. "Stress in Teenagers." MassGeneralBrigham. September 23, 2023. https://www.massgeneralbrigham.org/en/about/newsroom/arti cles/stress-in-teenagers.

Calm. "5, 4, 3, 2, 1 — A Simple Grounding Exercise to Calm Anxiety." Accessed September 17, 2024. https://www.calm.com/blog/5-4-3-2-1-a-simple-exer cise-to-calm-the-mind#:

Cincinnati Children's Hospital. "Common Pressures That Can Cause Stress in Teens." June 2022. https://www.cincinnatichildrens.org/health/t/teen-stres sors.

Cleveland Clinic. "Cortisol." Medically reviewed December 10, 2021. https://my. clevelandclinic.org/health/articles/22187-cortisol.

Dallas Cosmetic Dental. "10 Reasons Stress Management Matters." September 14, 2019. Dallas Cosmetic Dental (blog). https://dallascosmeticdental.com/10- real-reasons-stress-management-matters/.

Eilam, David, Rony Izhar, and Joel Mort. "Threat Detection: Behavioral Practices in Animals and Humans." Neuroscience & Biobehavioral Reviews/Neuroscience and Biobehavioral Reviews 35 (4): 999–1006. March 2011. https://doi.org/10.1016/j.neubiorev.2010.08.002.

gabevdesigns. "10 Effective Stress Management Techniques for Busy Professionals." Peace of Mind. Accessed September 17, 2024. https://peaceof mind4wellness.com/stress-management-techniques/.

Integris Health. "How Does Body Image Affect Mental Health?" May 26, 2022. https://integrishealth.org/resources/on-your-health/2022/may/how-does- body-image-affect-mental-health.

Lochrie, Amanda S., PhD. "What is Stress?" KidsHealth.org. Nemours Children's Health, Kids Health, Stress, For Teens. May 2023. https://kidshealth.org/en/ teens/stress.html.

Lyness, D'Arcy, PhD. "10 Ways to Manage Everyday Stress." Nemours TeensHealth. Nemours Children's Health. August 2022. https://kidshealth.org/ en/teens/stress-tips.html.

Mayo Clinic. "Stress Management." Overview. October 26, 2023. https://www. mayoclinic.org/tests-procedures/stress-management/about/pac-20384898.

RaisingChildren. "Stress and Stress Management: Pre-teens and teenagers." Accessed May 11, 2024. https://raisingchildren.net.au/pre-teens/mental- health-physical-health/stress-anxiety-depression/stress-in-teens.

ReachOut. "Stress in Teenagers." Stress and Teenagers. Accessed May 11, 2024. https://parents.au.reachout.com/common-concerns/everyday-issues/stress- and-teenagers.

Sanchez, Jonathon. "A Personal Perspective on Mental Health Awareness Month." Axios Charlotte. May 15, 2015. https://www.axios.com/local/charlotte/2015/05/15/a-personal-perspective-on-mental-health-awareness-month-3998.

Shrikant, Aditi. "Youth Suicide Rates Rose 62% from 2007 to 2021: 'People Feel Hopeless,' One Recent Grad Says." CNBC. Updated on December 7, 2023. https://www.cnbc.com/2023/12/05/youth-suicide-rates-rose-62percent-from-2007-to-2021.html.

Smith, Kathleen. "6 Common Triggers of Teen Stress." Health Central Corp. December 8, 2017. Updated on October 21, 2022. https://www.psycom.net/common-triggers-teen-stress.

"Stress Symptoms: Effects on Your Body and Behavior." Mayo Clinic. August 10, 2023. https://www.mayoclinic.org/healthy-lifestyle/stress-management/in-depth/stress-symptoms/art-20050987#:

"12 Ways to Manage Stress." Melbourne Polytechnic. November 10, 2019. https://www.melbournepolytechnic.edu.au/about-us/news-and-events/news/12-ways-to-manage-stress/.

University of Toledo. "Deep Breathing and Relaxation." Accessed September 17, 2024. https://www.utoledo.edu/studentaffairs/counseling/anxietytoolbox/breathingandrelaxation.html#:

Wikipedia. "The Dark Knight Rises." Accessed October 13, 2024. https://en.wikipedia.org/wiki/The_Dark_Knight_Rises.

World Health Organization. "Mental Health of Adolescents." November 17, 2021. https://www.who.int/news-room/fact-sheets/detail/adolescent-mental-health#:

SUPERPOWER #2: WELLNESS MANAGEMENT

CHRISTUS HWC. "Mastering Wellness and Fitness: The Ultimate Guide to Staying Motivated and Creating Healthy Habits." Wilton P. Hebert Wellness Center. June 27, 2023. https://christushwc.org/fitforlife/2023/mastering-wellness-and-fitness-the-ultimate-guide-to-staying-motivated-and-creating-healthy-habits.

Corporate Wellness Magazine.com. "Building a Personal Wellness Plan: A Step-by-Step Plan." Accessed September 23, 2024. https://www.corporatewellnessmagazine.com/article/building-a-personal-wellness-plan-a-step-by-step-guide.

Medium. "Anatomy of a Scene—The Training." August 15, 2022. https://benjweinberg.medium.com/anatomy-of-a-scene-the-training-bab3cebe95f1.

Quora. "If a Professional Nutritionist Built Batman's Diet, What Would It Look

Like?" Accessed October 29, 2024. https://www.quora.com/If-a-professional-nutritionist-built-Batman-s-diet-what-would-it-look-like.

EATING NUTRITIOUS FOOD

American Heart Association. "How to Reduce Sodium in Your Diet." Accessed September 21, 2024. https://www.heart.org/en/healthy-living/healthy-eating/eat-smart/sodium/how-to-reduce-sodium.

Barclay, Lily. "Best Recipes for Teenagers." Good Food. Accessed May 12, 2024. https://www.bbcgoodfood.com/howto/guide/recipes-teenagers.

Canada's Food Guide. "Healthy Cooking Methods." Modified July 21, 2021. https://food-guide.canada.ca/en/tips-for-healthy-eating/healthy-cooking-methods/.

Cleveland Clinic. "A Beginner's Guide to Healthy Meal Prep." HealthEssentials. January 15, 2014. https://health.clevelandclinic.org/a-beginners-guide-to-healthy-meal-prep.

Crichton-Stuart, Cathleen. "What Are the Benefits of Eating Healthy?" MedicalNewsToday. Updated on January 12, 2023. https://www.medicalnewstoday.com/articles/322268.

Flowater. "How Hydration Impacts Productivity in the Workplace." October 15, 2020. https://drinkflowater.com/how-hydration-impacts-productivity-in-the-workplace/.

Food Network. "40 Healthy Recipes the Whole Family Can Agree On." August 4, 2022. https://www.foodnetwork.com/recipes/photos/our-best-healthy-recipes-for-kids-and-families.

Gager, Erin. R.D. "Finding the Hidden Sugar in the Foods You Eat." Accessed September 21, 2024. https://www.hopkinsmedicine.org/health/wellness-and-prevention/finding-the-hidden-sugar-in-the-foods-you-eat.

Harvard Health Publishing. "Eating to Boost Energy." July 26, 2011. https://www.health.harvard.edu/healthbeat/eating-to-boost-energy#:

Harvard Health Publishing. "Foods Linked to Better Brain Power." Harvard Medical School. April 3, 2024. https://www.health.harvard.edu/healthbeat/foods-linked-to-better-brainpower.

Harvard Health Publishing. "How to Boost Your Immune System." March 28, 2024. https://www.health.harvard.edu/staying-healthy/how-to-boost-your-immune-system.

Harvard Health Publishing. "The Truth About Fats: The Good, the Bad, and the In-Between." April 12, 2022. https://www.health.harvard.edu/staying-healthy/the-truth-about-fats-bad-and-good.

Johns Hopkins Medicine. "Healthy Eating During Adolescence." Accessed May 11,

2024. https://www.hopkinsmedicine.org/health/wellness-and-prevention/
healthy-eating-during-adolescence.

John Muir Health. "Nutrition for Teens: Help your teenager develop a healthier
relationship with food." Accessed May 11, 2024. https://www.johnmuirhealth.
com/health-education/health-wellness/childrens-health/nutrition-teens.html.

Massachusetts General Hospital. "Have Healthy Snacks in Your Diet." Patient
Education. August 20, 2019. https://www.massgeneral.org/children/nutrition/
healthy-snacks-for-teens.

Mayo Clinic. "Bone Health: Tips to Keep Your Bones Healthy." December 3, 2022.
https://www.mayoclinic.org/healthy-lifestyle/adult-health/in-depth/bone-
health/art-20045060.

Mayo Clinic. "Dietary Fat: Know Which to Choose." Accessed October 1, 2024.
https://www.mayoclinic.org/healthy-lifestyle/nutrition-and-healthy-eating/
in-depth/fat/art-20045550.

Mayo Clinic. "Dietary Fiber: Essential for a Healthy Diet." November 4, 2022.
https://www.mayoclinic.org/healthy-lifestyle/nutrition-and-healthy-eating/
in-depth/fiber/art-20043983

McIntosh, James. "15 Benefits of Drinking Water." MedicalNewsToday. Updated
August 28, 2024. https://www.medicalnewstoday.com/articles/290814.

McIntosh, James. "What is Serotonin, and What Does It Do?" MedicalNewsToday.
Updated April 18, 2014. https://www.medicalnewstoday.com/articles/232248.

National Cancer Institute. "Antioxidants and Cancer Prevention." February 6,
2017. https://www.cancer.gov/about-cancer/causes-prevention/risk/diet/
antioxidants-fact-sheet.

Neuhauser, Marian L. "The Importance of Healthy Dietary Patterns in Chronic
Disease Prevention." National Library of Medicine. National Center for
Biotechnology Information. NIH. https://pubmed.ncbi.nlm.nih.gov/
30077352/.

Patwal, Swati. "27 Easy and Healthy Recipes for Teens to Cook."
MomJunction.com. Fact checked April 29, 2024. https://www.momjunction.
com/articles/easy-recipes-cooking-for-teenagers_00782578/.

Pearson, Keith. "How Omega-3 Fish Oil Affects Your Brain and Mental Health."
Healthline. July 25, 2023. https://www.healthline.com/nutrition/omega-3-
fish-oil-for-brain-health.

Robertson, Ruairi, PhD. 2020. "The Gut-Brain Connection: How It Works and the
Role of Nutrition." Healthline. August 20, 2020. https://www.healthline.com/
nutrition/gut-brain-connection.

Tinsley, Grant. "26 Foods to Eat to Build Muscle." Healthline. Updated February
15, 2024. https://www.healthline.com/nutrition/26-muscle-building-foods.

EXERCISING REGULARLY

Better Health Channel. "Physical Activity: It's important." Reviewed on November 17, 2023. https://www.betterhealth.vic.gov.au/health/healthyliving/physical-activity-its-important.

Center for Disease Control and Prevention. "Benefits of Physical Activity." Reviewed August 1, 2023. https://www.cdc.gov/physicalactivity/basics/pa-health/index.htm.

Centers for Disease Control and Prevention. "Youth Physical Activity Guidelines." Reviewed on July 26, 2022. https://www.cdc.gov/healthyschools/physicalactivity/guidelines.htm

Clifton, Tamera CPT. "Exercise of Teenagers: A complete guide." Healthline.com. April 13, 2022. https://www.healthline.com/health/fitness/exercise-for-teenagers#bottom-line.

Cox, Carla. "Role of Physical Activity for Weight Loss and Weight Maintenance." National Library of Medicine. National Center for Biotechnology Information. NIH. August 2017. https://www.ncbi.nlm.nih.gov/pmc/articles/PMC5556592/.

Gomez-Penilla, Fernando, and Charles Hillman. "The Influence of Exercise on Cognitive Abilities." National Library of Medicine. National Center for Biotechnology Information. NIH. January 2013. https://www.ncbi.nlm.nih.gov/pmc/articles/PMC3951958/.

Harvard Health. "Exercising to Relax." July 7, 2020. https://www.health.harvard.edu/staying-healthy/exercising-to-relax#:

Healthi. "How to Make Physical Activity an Enjoyable Part of Your Lifestyle." May 9, 2023. https://blog.healthiapp.com/article/how-to-make-physical-activity-an-enjoyable-part-of-your-lifestyle/.

Hinge Health. "12 Bodyweight Exercises PTs Want You to Try." Hinge Health Learning Center. Hinge Health, Inc. September 17, 2024. https://www.hingehealth.com/resources/articles/bodyweight-exercises/.

Mayo Clinic. "Walking: Trim Your Waistline, Improve Your Health." Healthy Lifestyle. Fitness. March 12, 2024. https://www.mayoclinic.org/healthy-lifestyle/fitness/in-depth/walking/art-20046261.

MedicinePlus. "Benefits of Exercise." National Library of Medicine. NIH. Accessed September 22, 2024. https://medlineplus.gov/benefitsofexercise.html.

St. Jude Children's Research Hospital. "Physical Activity for Teens and 20s." Together. August 2020. https://together.stjude.org/en-us/teensand20s/take-care-of-yourself/physical-activity.html.

Wikipedia. "High-Intensity Interval Training." Accessed September 22, 2024. https://en.wikipedia.org/wiki/High-intensity_interval_training.

World Health Organization. "Physical Activity." October 5, 2022. https://www. who.int/news-room/fact-sheets/detail/physical-activity.

GETTING ENOUGH SLEEP

Bryan, Lucy, and Brandon Peters. "Why Do We Need Sleep?" Sleep Foundation. Updated April 5, 2024. https://www.sleepfoundation.org/how-sleep-works/ why-do-we-need-sleep.

Center for Disease Control and Prevention. "Tips for Better Sleep." Reviewed September 13, 2022. https://www.cdc.gov/sleep/about_sleep/sleep_hygien e.html.

Cleveland Clinic. "Sleep." Reviewed September 19, 2023. https://my.cleveland clinic.org/health/body/12148-sleep-basics.

Johns Hopkins Medicine. "Why Sleep Is Important for Teens." Accessed September 17, 2024. https://www.hopkinsmedicine.org/all-childrens-hospital/services/ pediatric-and-adolescent-medicine/healthy-weight-initiative/ages-12-17/ why-sleep-is-important-for-teens.

Lewis, Penelope A., Gunther Knoblich, and Gina Poe. "How Memory Replay in Sleep Boosts Creative Problem-Solving." National Library of Medicine. National Center for Biotechnology Information. NIH. June 2018. https:// www.ncbi.nlm.nih.gov/pmc/articles/PMC7543772/.

National Heart, Lung, and Blood Institute. "How Sleep Works: Why is Sleep Important?" National Institutes of Health. Updated March 24, 2022. https:// www.nhlbi.nih.gov/health/sleep/why-sleep-important.

Newsom, Rob, and Abhinav Singh. "Blue Light: What It Is and How It Affects Sleep." Sleep Foundation. January 12, 2024. https://www.sleepfoundation.org/ bedroom-environment/blue-light.

Nieto, Aaron. "The Importance of Sleep During the Teen Years." Baylor College of Medicine. August 3, 2023. https://www.bcm.edu/news/the-importance-of- sleep-during-the-teen-years.

Suni, Eric, and Alex Dimitriu. "Teens and Sleep: An overview of why teens face unique sleep challenges and tips to help them sleep better." Sleep Foundation. Updated October 4, 2023. https://www.sleepfoundation.org/teens-and-sleep.

Suni, Eric, and Rosen, David. "Mastering Sleep Hygiene: Your Path to Quality Sleep." Sleep Foundation. Updated March 4, 2024. https://www.sleepfounda tion.org/sleep-hygiene.

Vandekerckhove, Marie, and Yu-lin Wang. "Emotion, Emotion Regulation, and Sleep: An Intimate Relationship." National Library of Medicine. National Center for Biotechnology Information. NIH. December 1, 2017. https://www. ncbi.nlm.nih.gov/pmc/articles/PMC7181893/.

SUPERPOWER #3: SELF-REFLECTION

Davis, Tchiki. "Self-Reflection: Definition and How to Do It." The Berkeley Well-Being Institute. Accessed September 17, 2024. https://www.berkeleywellbeing.com/what-is-self-reflection.html.

Fandom. "Rachel Dawes." Dark Knight Wiki. Accessed October 13, 2024. https://nolan-batman.fandom.com/wiki/Rachel_Dawes.

Gupta, Sanjana. "The Importance of Self-Reflection: How Looking Inward Can Improve Your Mental Health." VeryWell Mind. May 25, 2023. https://www.verywellmind.com/self-reflection-importance-benefits-and-strategies-7500858.

Perry, Elizabeth. "Get to Know Yourself Through the Act of Self-Reflection." BetterUp. December 21, 2022. https://www.betterup.com/blog/self-reflection.

SUPERPOWER #4: MINDFULNESS

Batts, Alex. "Men Are Still Good: An Analysis of Batman in 'Batman v Superman.'" CinemaDebate. March 21, 2019. https://cinemadebate.com/2019/03/21/men-are-still-good-an-analysis-of-batman-in-batman-v-superman/.

Capecchi, Stephanie, and Saleh Naveed, MD. "Mindfulness for Teens: How It Works, Benefits, & 11 Exercises to Try." Choosing Therapy, Inc. June 8, 2022. https://www.choosingtherapy.com/mindfulness-for-teens/.

Chemin. "5-4-3-2-1 Method." September 14, 2021. https://maisonchemin.com/blogs/articles/if-you-have-panic-attacks-try-this-easy-technique.

Cherry, Kendra. "Benefits of Mindfulness." Verywell Mind. September 2, 2022. https://www.verywellmind.com/the-benefits-of-mindfulness-5205137.

Garey, Juliann. "The Power of Mindfulness." Child Mind Institute, Inc. May 15, 2024. https://childmind.org/article/the-power-of-mindfulness/

HelpGuide.org. "Benefits of Mindfulness." Accessed October 3, 2024. https://www.helpguide.org/mental-health/stress/benefits-of-mindfulness.

Hoshaw, Crystal. "What is Mindfulness? A Simple Practice for Greater Wellbeing." Healthline.com. March 29, 2022. https://www.healthline.com/health/mind-body/what-is-mindfulness#benefits.

Knowles, Ashleigh. "100 Mindfulness Activities for Teens, Worksheets, & Questions." CarePatron. February 29, 2024. https://www.carepatron.com/guides/mindfulness-activities-for-teens.

MoniqueTalon. "10 Simple Ways to Practice Mindfulness in Our Daily Life." April 13, 2020. https://moniquetallon.com/10-simple-ways-to-practice-mindfulness-in-our-daily-life/.

CHAPTER 2: CORE PERSONAL DEVELOPMENT

Bond, Scott. "What Spider-Man Can Teach Us About Responsibility as Leaders." LinkedIn. July 21, 2019. https://www.linkedin.com/pulse/what-spider-man-can-teach-us-responsibility-leaders-scott-bond/.

Thompson, Whitney. "Week Five—Spider-Man Learning 'With Great Power Comes Great Responsibility.'" Anchor Counseling Centers. November 15, 2022. https://www.anchorcounselingcenters.com/superhero-blog/week-5-spider-man-learning-with-great-power-comes-great-responsibility.

SUPERPOWER #5: PERSONAL RESPONSIBILITY

Bennett, Michelle. "What Does It Mean to Take Responsibility for Your Actions at Work?" Niagara Institute, Inc. June 9, 2021. https://www.niagarainstitute.com/blog/take-responsibility-for-your-actions.

Course Hero. "Ways on How to Become a Responsible Adolescent Prepared for Adult Life." Learneo, Inc. April 17, 2021. https://www.coursehero.com/file/88968512/Ways-on-how-to-become-a-Responsible-Adolescent-prepared-for-Adult-Lifedocx/.

Fandom. "Peter Parker." Accessed October 13, 2024. https://marvel.fandom.com/wiki/Peter_Parker_(Earth-616).

Finkelstein, Darren. "What Is Personal Responsibility?" Tick Those Boxes. Accessed September 17, 2024. https://tickthoseboxes.com.au/what-is-personal-responsibility/.

High 5 Test. "Personal Responsibility: What It Is, Examples and How to Develop & Improve." Accessed May 13, 2024. https://high5test.com/personal-responsibility/.

Intecor. "Self-Responsibility: A Daily Challenge with Explosive Benefits." July 11, 2019. https://itecor.com/self-responsibility-a-daily-challenge-with-explosive-benefits/.

Life and Progress. "Taking Responsibility and Ownership." Accessed October 12, 2024. https://www.lifeandprogress.co.uk/latest-news/taking-responsibility-and-ownership/#:

Master Class. "How to Take Responsibility for Your Actions." May 17, 2022. https://www.masterclass.com/articles/taking-responsibility-for-your-actions.

Matijasevic, Marko. "Self-Responsibility: Deeply Needed Skill in Today's Age." Markoo.com. November 19, 2023. https://markooo.com/self-responsibility/.

Parker, Kirsten, MFA. "How to Be a Responsible Teen." WikiHow. Updated October 7, 2023. https://www.wikihow.com/Be-a-Responsible-Teen.

Prakash, Vaishali. "Responsible Citizenship: An Essential Element for a Better

Society." SarvaYog. June 13, 2023. https://www.sarvayog.com/responsible-citi zenship-an-essential-element-for-a-better-society/.

Thompson, Whitney. "Week Five—Spider-Man Learning 'With Great Power Comes Great Responsibility." Anchor Counseling Centers. November 15, 2022. https://www.anchorcounselingcenters.com/superhero-blog/week-5-spider-man-learning-with-great-power-comes-great-responsibility.

YMCA. "24 Volunteer Ideas for Teens." YMCA. March 16, 2021. https://www.ymca.org/ystories/youth-teen-development/24-volunteer-ideas-for-teens.

SUPERPOWER #6: STRATEGIC THINKING

Angelo, Lindsay. "What is Strategic Thinking? Explained..." Accessed September 23, 2024. https://lindsayangelo.com/thinkingcont/what-is-strategic-thinking.

Asana, Inc. "What Are Smart Goals: Examples and Templates." February 23, 2024. https://asana.com/resources/smart-goals.

Bell, Simon. "SMART Goals." Mind Tools. Accessed October 12, 2024. https://www.mindtools.com/a4wo118/smart-goals.

BetterHelp. "10 Ways Driving Ambition May Help You Succeed." Updated April 16, 2024. https://www.betterhelp.com/advice/ambition/10-ways-driving-ambition-helps-you-succeed-sometimes/.

Boys & Girls Clubs of America. "The Importance of Goal-Setting for Teens." Parent Resources. January 19, 2022. https://www.bgca.org/news-stories/2022/January/the-importance-of-goal-setting-for-teens.

Bridges, Jennifer. "How to Write an Inspiring Personal Vision Statement." Reputation Defender by Norton. September 22, 2020. https://www.reputation defender.com/blog/job-seekers/how-to-write-an-inspiring-personal-vision-statement.

BusinessThink. "What Are the 6 P's of Strategic Thinking." BusinessThink. Accessed September 17, 2024. https://businessthink.in/what-are-the-6-ps-of-strategic-thinking/

Center for Management and Organizational Effectiveness. "Strategic Thinking." Accessed May 16, 2024. https://cmoe.com/glossary/strategic-thinking/.

Imbastoni, Giulia. "Four Steps to Create a Personal Vision Statement and Change Your Life." BetterUp. May 5, 2023. https://www.betterup.com/blog/create-a-personal-vision-statement.

IMDB. "Spider-Man: Homecoming Plot." Accessed October 13. 2024. https://www.imdb.com/title/tt2250912/plotsummary/.

Kaplan, Soren. "Elevate Your Leadership: Unleashing the Power of Strategic Thinking." Accessed September 29, 2024. https://www.sorenkaplan.com/strate gic-thinking-for-leaders/.

LogicLike. "Strategic Thinking: What It Is, Why it Matters, and How to Improve." Accessed May 16, 2024. https://logiclike.com/en/blog/strategic-thinking.

MyTutor. "The Psychology of Goal Setting: How to Help Teens Set Effective Goals." Blog/For Parents/Educational Advice. Accessed May 14, 2024. https://www.mytutor.co.uk/blog/parents/educational-advice/goal-setting-for-teens/.

O'Byrne, Ian W. PhD. "Developing a Personal Vision Statement." Wiobyrne. February 13, 2018. https://wiobyrne.com/vision-statement/.

Ramamoorthy, Archana, and Amy Bobinger. "10+ Ways to Improve Your Strategic Thinking Skills." WikiHow. Updated July 8, 2022. https://www.wikihow.com/Improve-Your-Strategy.

Smith, Hayley Vaughn. "SMART Goals for Teens: What Does SMART Mean? (Parent Guide)." They Are The Future. Accessed May 14, 2024. https://www.theyarethefuture.co.uk/smart-goals-teens/.

Tritsch, Erik. "How to Set Goals for Teens: The SMART Goals Method." Fairborn Digital Academy. January 31, 2022. https://fairborndigital.us/2022/01/01/smart-goals-for-teens/.

Your Therapy Source. "Smart Goals for Teens." Accessed May 14, 2024. https://www.yourtherapysource.com/blog1/2022/08/11/smart-goals-for-teens-3/.

SUPERPOWER #7: RESILIENCE

Barry, Sean. "'Spider-Man: Far From Home' and Seeing Beyond the Illusions." The Jesuit Post. July 12, 2019. https://thejesuitpost.org/2019/07/spider-man-far-from-home-and-seeing-beyond-the-illusions/.

Calm. "How to Become More Resilient: 8 Ways to Build Your Resilience." Accessed September 23, 2024. https://www.calm.com/blog/how-to-be-resilient.

Duszynski-Goodman, Lizzie. "What Is Resilience? How to Build It, Benefits and More." Forbes. Updated April 17, 2024. https://www.forbes.com/health/mind/resilience/.

Mayo Clinic. "Resilience: Build Skills to Endure Hardship." December 23, 2023. https://www.mayoclinic.org/tests-procedures/resilience-training/in-depth/resilience/art-20046311.

White-Gibson, Zuri. "Resilience in Teens: Customizing Your Mental Toolkit." PsychCentral. Updated June 21, 2022. https://psychcentral.com/health/tips-to-build-resilience-in-teens-and-young-adults#resilience-defined.

SUPERPOWER #8: CREATIVITY

Birt, Jamie. "18 Creativity Exercises to Improve Creative Thinking at Work." Indeed. August 15, 2024. https://www.indeed.com/career-advice/career-devel opment/creativity-exercise.

Newport Academy. "The Link Between Creativity and Mental Health." Teen Mental Health & Substance Abuse Treatment Centers. November 28, 2018. https://www.newportacademy.com/resources/empowering-teens/creativity-and-mental-health/.

Psychology Today. "Creativity." Accessed May 15, 2024. https://www.psychology today.com/us/basics/creativity.

Wikipedia. "Spider-Man: No Way Home." Accessed October 13, 2024. https://en. wikipedia.org/wiki/Spider-Man:_No_Way_Home.

Wooll, Maggie, MBA. "What is Creative Thinking and How Can I Improve?" BetterUp. June 14, 2024. https://www.betterup.com/blog/creative-thinking.

Yonobi. "10 Reasons Why Creativity Is Important." YONOBI (blog). January 1, 2023. https://yonobi.com/blogs/news/being-creative-and-why-its-important-for-our-well-being.

CHAPTER 3: ANALYTICAL AND DECISION-MAKING SKILLS

Marvel Cinematic Universe. "Iron Man." Fandom. Accessed September 23, 2024. https://marvelcinematicuniverse.fandom.com/wiki/Iron_Man.

Wikipedia. "Iron Man." Accessed September 23, 2024. https://en.wikipedia.org/wiki/Iron_Man.

SUPERPOWER #9: ANALYTICAL SKILLS

IMDB. "Iron Man: Plot." Accessed October 13, 2024. https://m.imdb.com/title/tt0371746/plotsummary/.

Indeed. "10 Ways to Improve Your Analytical Skills." Updated February 3, 2023. https://www.indeed.com/career-advice/career-development/improve-analyti cal-skills.

Indeed. "What Are Analytical Skills? Definition, Examples and Tips." Updated June 22, 2023. https://www.indeed.com/career-advice/resumes-cover-letters/analytical-skills.

Kaplan, Zoe. "What Are Analytical Skills? Definition and Examples." Forage. Updated April 13, 2023. April 13, 2023. https://www.theforage.com/blog/skills/analytical-skills.

TWProject. "Analytical Skills for Successful Projects." Accessed September 17, 2021. https://twproject.com/blog/analytical-skills-successful-projects/.

Ward, Shauna. "What Is a Mind Map? Tips, Examples, and Templates." Mural. August 30, 2023. https://www.mural.co/blog/mind-mapping.

SUPERPOWER #10: CRITICAL THINKING

Boris. "Be a Better Thinker with These 7 Critical Thinking Exercises." ABLE Blog: Thoughts, Learnings and Experiences. June 6, 2022. https://able.ac/blog/critical-thinking-exercises/.

Doerr, Joseph. "Questioning Your Assumptions: Why It's Important for Your Personal and Professional Growth." LinkedIn. February 23, 2023. https://www.linkedin.com/pulse/questioning-your-assumptions-why-its-important-growth-doerr-cris.

Handel, Steven. "Playing Devil's Advocate with Negative Beliefs: The Power of Proving Yourself Wrong." The Emotion Machine. Accessed September 23, 2024. https://www.theemotionmachine.com/playing-devils-advocate-with-negative-beliefs-the-power-of-proving-yourself-wrong/.

Indeed. "A Guide to Critical Thinking Steps (With Benefits and Tips)." June 27, 2024. https://ca.indeed.com/career-advice/career-development/critical-thinking-steps.

Marvel Cinematic Universe Wiki. "Iron Man." Accessed October 13, 2024. https://marvelcinematicuniverse.fandom.com/wiki/Iron_Man.

SkillsYouNeed. "The Best Ways to Improve Your Critical Thinking Skills." Accessed May 25, 2024. https://www.skillsyouneed.com/rhubarb/improve-critical-thinking.html.

University of Michigan. "Fake News and Critical Thinking in the Post-truth World." October 2022. https://globalchange.umich.edu/globalchange1/current/lectures/kling/fake_news/fake_news.html.

Wikipedia. "Iron Man 2." Accessed October 13, 2024. https://en.wikipedia.org/wiki/Iron_Man_2.

SUPERPOWER #11: PROBLEM-SOLVING SKILLS

CC/MIT. "What Is Problem Solving and Why Is It Important?" Introduction to Problem Solving Skills. MIT Office of Digital Learning. Accessed May 25, 2024. https://ccmit.mit.edu/problem-solving/.

Liles, Maryn. "50 Lateral Thinking Puzzles That'll Stretch Your Mind in a Whole New Way." Parade. Updated October 31, 2023. https://parade.com/1288259/marynliles/lateral-thinking-puzzles/#:

Never Felt Better. "Review: Iron Man 3." May 3, 2013. https://neverfeltbetter. wordpress.com/2013/05/03/review-iron-man-3/.

SessionLab. "40 Problem-Solving Techniques and Processes." June 25, 2024. https://www.sessionlab.com/blog/problem-solving-techniques/.

Youth Empowerment. "How to Use Skills to Logically Solve a Problem." Accessed May 25, 2024. https://youthempowerment.com/problem-solving/.

SUPERPOWER #12: DECISION-MAKING SKILLS

Griffin, Trudi. "How to Improve Your Decision-Making Skills." WikiHow. September 25, 2023. https://www.wikihow.com/Improve-Your-Decision-Making-Skills.

Han, Esther. "7 Ways to Improve Your Ethical Decision-Making." Harvard Business School Online. Business Insights. August 3, 2023. https://online.hbs. edu/blog/post/ethical-decision-making-process.

Herrity, Jennifer. "Decision-Making Skills: Definitions and Examples." Indeed. Updated August 15, 2024. https://www.indeed.com/career-advice/career-development/decision-making-skills.

Laoyan, Sarah. "7 Important Steps in the Decision Making Process." Asana, Inc. January 17, 2024. https://asana.com/resources/decision-making-process.

Lucidchart. "7 Steps of the Decision-Making Process." Accessed May 25, 2024. https://www.lucidchart.com/blog/decision-making-process-steps.

MasterClass. "How to Make Informed Decisions: 7 Step Decision-Making Process." Updated June 7, 2021. https://www.masterclass.com/articles/how-to-make-informed-decisions.

Umass Dartmouth. "Decision-making Process." Accessed September 17, 2014. https://www.umassd.edu/fycm/decision-making/process/,

University of Massachusetts, Dartmouth. "Decision-Making Process: 7 Steps to Effective Decision Making." Accessed May 25, 2024. https://www.umassd.edu/fycm/decision-making/process/.

Wikipedia. "Avengers: Endgame." Accessed October 13, 2024. https://en.wiki pedia.org/wiki/Avengers:_Endgame.

CHAPTER 4: COMMUNICATIONS AND INTERPERSONAL SKILLS

Wikipedia. "Wonder Woman." Accessed September 24, 2024. https://en.wikipedia. org/wiki/Wonder_Woman.

SUPERPOWER #13 COMMUNICATION SKILLS

Ackerman, Courtney E. "49 Communication Activities, Exercises, & Games." Positive Psychology. May 27, 2019. https://positivepsychology.com/communi cation-games-and-activities/.

Buckner, Lotus. "What Is Effective Communication? (With Benefits and Tips)." Indeed. Updated August 15, 2024. https://www.indeed.com/career-advice/ career-development/effective-communication.

CFI Education, Inc. "Communication Skills: Transferring Information to Produce a Greater Understanding." Accessed May 25, 2024. https://corporatefinancein stitute.com/resources/management/communication/.

Cleveland Clinic. "7 Ways to Improve Your Active Listening Skills." HealthEssentials. May 24, 2023. https://health.clevelandclinic.org/active-listening.

Coursera. "What Is Effective Communications? Skills for Work, School, and Life." Updated May 22, 2024. https://www.coursera.org/articles/communication-effectiveness.

Cuncic, Arlin. "7 Active Listening Techniques for Better Communication." Verywell Mind. Dotdash Media, Inc. Updated February 12, 2024. https://www. verywellmind.com/what-is-active-listening-3024343.

Hollander, Alan. "Average Human Attention Span by Age: 60 Statistics." Bridge Care. September 14, 2023. https://www.bridgecareaba.com/blog/average-human-attention-span#:

Martines, Alanna. "Wonder Woman 2017: Wonder Woman as a Sign of Feminism." OpenOregon. Accessed October 13, 2024. https://openoregon.pressbooks. pub/dpdfilm/chapter/wonder-woman-2017/.

Mikula, Joanne. "Wonder Woman: Female Strength and the Power of Love." *The Bi-College News*. December 2, 2017. https://bicollegenews.com/2017/12/02/ wonder-woman-female-strength-and-the-power-of-love/.

Saavedra, Justine. "Communication Skills: Definition, Examples, & Activities." Berkeley Well-Being Institute. Accessed May 25, 2024. https://www.berkeley wellbeing.com/communication-skills.html.

Segal, Jeanne, PhD, Melinda Smith, Lawrence Robinson, and Greg Boose. "Body Language and Nonverbal Communication: Communicating Without Words." HelpGuide. Reviewed May 8, 2024. https://www.helpguide.org/articles/rela tionships-communication/nonverbal-communication.htm.

SkillsYouNeed. "Communication Skills." Accessed May 25, 2024. https://www. skillsyouneed.com/ips/communication-skills.html#google_vignette.

Vyas, Tanvi. "Nonverbal Communication: The Importance of Body Language and

Tone." LinkedIn. May 23, 2023. https://www.linkedin.com/pulse/nonverbal-communication-importance-body-language-tone-tanvi-vyas.

Wyatt, A. C. "Wonder Woman 2017 Movie Review: In Dianna Prince, Complexity, and Strength." Medium. July 28, 2017. https://medium.com/@novelramblings/wonder-woman-review-diana-complexity-strength-b3ba6ab5f2cb.

SUPERPOWER #14: INTERPERSONAL SKILLS

Aman, Jodi. "How to Teach Empathy to Your Teen—And Why They Will Thank You." DoctorJodi. Accessed June 6, 2024. https://jodiaman.com/blog/teach-empathy-to-your-teen/.

Coursera. "What Are Interpersonal Skills? And How to Strengthen Them." Updated January 31, 2024. https://www.coursera.org/articles/interpersonal-skills.

Manson, Mark. "3 Core Components of a Healthy Relationship." Mark Manson. Accessed June 6, 2024. https://markmanson.net/3-core-components-of-a-healthy-relationship.

Marriage In A Box. "Trust and Respect Are the Key to a Healthy Relationship." March 8, 2019. https://www.marriageinabox.com/blog/trust-and-respect-are-the-key-to-a-healthy-relationship/.

Model United Nations. "Model United Nations." Accessed September 24, 2024. https://www.un.org/en/mun.

Poorkavoos, Meysam. "Eight Behaviors That Build Trust." Roffey Park Institute. Accessed September 24, 2024. https://www.roffeypark.com/articles/eight-behaviours-that-build-trust/.

Reid, Sheldon. "Empathy: How to Feel and Respond to the Emotions of Others." HelpGuide. Accessed June 6, 2024. https://www.helpguide.org/relationships/communication/empathy.

SkillsYouNeed. "Interpersonal Skills." Accessed May 26, 2024. https://www.skillsyouneed.com/interpersonal-skills.html.

SUPERPOWER #15: NEGOTIATING SKILLS

Board Game Geek. "Negotiation Games: Your Favourites and Why." Edited June 18, 2013. https://boardgamegeek.com/geeklist/158560/negotiation-games-your-favourites-and-why.

The Big Red Group. "Mastering the Art of Negotiation for Teens!" July 23, 2022. https://www.thebigredgroup.com/mastering-the-art-of-negotiation-for-teens/.

Dodge, Amanda. "Why Your Students Need Strong Negotiating Skills." Ozobot.

October 29, 2019. https://ozobot.com/why-your-students-need-strong-negoti ation-skills/.

MiddleEarth. "The Importance of Negotiation Skills for Adolescents." August 5, 2019. https://middleearthnj.org/2019/08/05/the-importance-of-negotiation-skills-for-adolescents/.

SkillsYouNeed. "What Is Negotiation?" Accessed June 7, 2024. https://www.skillsy ouneed.com/ips/negotiation.html.

SUPERPOWER #16: CONFLICT RESOLUTION

eSoft Online Training Solutions. "Effective Guide to Conflict Resolution for Teenagers." Accessed June 7, 2024. https://esoftskills.com/conflict-resolution-for-teens/.

Everyday Speech. "Promoting Harmony: Conflict Resolution Techniques for High School Students." Accessed June 7, 2024. https://everydayspeech.com/sel-implementation/promoting-harmony-conflict-resolution-techniques-for-high-school-students/.

Glaser, Bradford R. "7 of Our Favorite Conflict Resolution Games and Activities." HRDQ. February 8, 2022. https://hrdqstore.com/blogs/hrdq-blog/conflict-resolution-games-activities?srsltid=AfmBOooePyGbzY9kSf2lHQFSw4bFdjf YUTIdTXFdfyWvbpAVixYBdyLI.

Modern Recovery. "Conflict Resolution: Definition, Benefits & Techniques." July 26, 2023. https://modernrecoveryservices.com/wellness/coping/skills/social/ conflict-resolution/.

Vallejo, Michael, "A Guide for Conflict Resolution for Teens." Mental Health Center Kids. November 1, 2023. https://mentalhealthcenterkids.com/blogs/ articles/conflict-resolution-for-teens.

CHAPTER 5: LEADERSHIP AND TEAMWORK

Adler, Cindy Rella. "Why Captain America Is the Leadership Role Model You Didn't Know You Needed." LinkedIn. January 31, 2019. https://www.linkedin. com/pulse/why-captain-america-leadership-role-model-you-didnt-know-cindy-adler.

Lady Spain. "Superheroes Inspirational Quotes." Oh My Fiesta! For Geeks. Accessed October 30, 2024. https://bit.ly/3C5FSIr

Wallace, Bill. "10 Leadership Secrets from Captain America." Selling Power. November 11, 2014. https://www.sellingpower.com/blog/10-leadership-secrets-from-captain-america.

SUPERPOWER #17: LEADERSHIP SKILLS

The Big Red Group. "10 Ways to Develop Leadership Skills as a Teen." March 24, 2022. https://www.thebigredgroup.com/10-ways-you-can-develop-leadership-skills-as-a-teen/.

IMDB. "Captain America: The Winter Soldier." Plot. Summaries. Accessed October 13, 2024. https://www.imdb.com/title/tt1843866/plotsummary/.

Martins, Julia. "How to Lead by Example, According to One Asana Leader." Asana, Inc. January 30, 2024. https://asana.com/resources/lead-by-example.

Pandey, Nikhil. "What Is Leadership? Definition, Meaning & Importance." Emeritus India. May 9, 2024. https://emeritus.org/in/learn/what-is-leadership/.

Spirit, Michelle. "The 5 Steps of Leadership Process in Business." LinkedIn. December 11, 2023. https://www.linkedin.com/pulse/5-steps-leadership-process-business-michelle-spirit-2ggce/.

Van De Hey, Ethan. "The Power of Positive Reinforcement." LinkedIn. January 28, 2023. https://www.linkedin.com/pulse/power-positive-reinforcement-ethan-van-de-hey.

SUPERPOWER #18: EMOTIONAL INTELLIGENCE

Cherry, Kendra. "Emotional Intelligence: How We Perceive, Evaluate, Express, and Control Emotions." Verywell Mind. Dotdash Media, Inc. Dotdash Merideth. Updated January 31, 2024. https://www.verywellmind.com/what-is-emotional-intelligence-2795423.

Cherry, Kendra. "5 Key Emotional Intelligence Skills." Verywell Mind. Dotdash Media, Inc. Dotdash Merideth. December 31, 2023. https://www.verywellmind.com/components-of- emotional-intelligence-2795438.

Moulton, Mike. "Journaling for Success: Enhancing Emotional Intelligence." LinkedIn. October 2, 2023. https://www.linkedin.com/pulse/journaling-success-enhancing-emotional-intelligence-mike/.

Roche Martin (UK) Ltd. "50 Tips for Improving Your Emotional Intelligence." Inspired Emotional Intelligence. January 12, 2022. https://www.rochemartin.com/blog/50-tips-improving-emotional-intelligence.

Sudbrink, Laurie. "Emotional Intelligence Is an Important Part of Strong Leadership." Business Leadership Today, LLC. Accessed June 7, 2024. https://businessleadershiptoday.com/emotional-intelligence-is-an-important-part-of-strong-leadership/.

Wikipedia. "Captain America: Civil War." Accessed October 13, 2024. https://en.wikipedia.org/wiki/Captain_America:_Civil_War.

SUPERPOWER #19: TEAMWORK

GGI Insights. "Teamwork Skills: Enhancing Collaboration and Productivity at Work." Gray Group International. August 6, 2024. https://www.graygroupintl.com/blog/teamwork-skills.

HyperTech, Inc. "What Is Teamwork: Definition, Meaning." Weje. Accessed June 8, 2024. https://weje.io/blog/what-is-teamwork.

IMDB. "The Avengers." Plot. Summaries. Accessed October 13, 2024. https://www.imdb.com/title/tt0848228/plotsummary/.

Perry, Elizabeth. "What Will Make or Break Your Next Role? Find Out Why Teamwork Matters." BetterUp. April 7, 2022. https://www.betterup.com/blog/what-is-teamwork.

SUPERPOWER #20: RESPONSIBLE CITIZENSHIP

Heldt, Aaron. "The Importance of Community Service in a Teen's Life." The Bridge Teen Center. February 17, 2021. https://thebridgeteencenter.org/news/the-importance-of-community-service-in-a-teens-life.

Hussey, Sally. "Why Is Community Engagement Important?" Granicus. Accessed June 8, 2024. https://granicus.com/blog/why-is-community-engagement-important/.

IMDB. "Captain America: The First Avenger." Plot. Summaries. Accessed October 13, 2024. https://www.imdb.com/title/tt0458339/plotsummary/.

Latham, M. "Young Volunteers: The Benefits of Community Service." University of Nevada, Reno Extension. 2003. https://extension.unr.edu/publication.aspx?PubID=4307.

Prakash, Vaishali. "Responsible Citizenship: An Essential Element for a Better Society." SarvaYog. June 13, 2023. https://www.sarvayog.com/responsible-citizenship-an-essential-element-for-a-better-society/.

Schwartz, Marie. "50 Community Service Ideas for Teen Volunteers." TeenLife. October 24, 2023. https://www.teenlife.com/blog/50-community-service-ideas-teen-volunteers/.

YMCA of the USA. "24 Volunteer Ideas for Teens." The Y. March 16, 2021. https://www.ymca.org/blog/articles/24-volunteer-ideas-for-teens.

CHAPTER 6: PRACTICAL LIFE MANAGEMENT

Marvel. "Black Widow (Natasha Romanoff) on Screen Powers, Villains, History." Accessed September 17, 2024. https://www.marvel.com/characters/black-widow-natasha-romanoff/on-screen.

Marvel. "Natasha Romanova: Black Widow." Accessed June 9, 2024. https://www.
marvel.com/characters/black-widow-natasha-romanova/in-comics.

SUPERPOWER #21: HABIT MANAGEMENT

American Heart Association. "How to Break Bad Habits and Change Behaviors."
Reviewed December 14, 2023. https://www.heart.org/en/healthy-living/
healthy-lifestyle/mental-health-and-wellbeing/how-to-break-bad-habits-and-
change-behaviors.

Arlinghaus, Katherine, and Craig A. Johnston. "The Importance of Creating Habits
and Routines." National Library of Medicine. National Center of
Biotechnology Information. NIH. December 29, 2018. https://www.ncbi.nlm.
nih.gov/pmc/articles/PMC6378489/.

Calm. "How Long Does It Take to Create a Habit (And How to Do It)?" Accessed
October 18, 2024. https://www.calm.com/blog/how-long-does-it-take-to-
create-a-habit

Clear, James. *Atomic Habits: An Easy & Proven Way to Build Good Habits and Break
Bad Ones.* Avery, an imprint of Penguin Random House. 2018.

Clear, James. "The Habits Guide: How to Build Good Habits and Break Bad Ones."
James Clear. Accessed June 9, 2024. https://jamesclear.com/habits.

Clear, James. "How to Build New Habits by Taking Advantage of Old Ones."
Excerpt from *Atomic Habits* by James Clear. Accessed June 9, 2024. https://
jamesclear.com/habit-stacking.

Cleveland Clinic. "How to Break Bad Habits." December 29, 2023. https://health.
clevelandclinic.org/how-to-break-bad-habits

Daoire, Noelle. "Habit vs. Routine: What's the Difference." Shimmer. December 8,
2023. https://www.shimmer.care/blog/habit-vs-routine

Davis, Tchiki. "Habits (Good & Bad): Definition, Books & Tips." Berkeley Well-
Being Institute. https://www.berkeleywellbeing.com/habits.html.

Gardner, Benjamin, Phillippa Lally, and Jane Wardle. "Making Health Habitual:
The Psychology of 'Habit Formation' and General Practice." National Library
of Medicine. National Center of Biotechnology Information. NIH. December
2012. https://pmc.ncbi.nlm.nih.gov/articles/PMC3505409/

Seaver, Maggie. "Habit Stacking Makes New Habits Last: Here's How It Works."
Real Simple. Dotdash Merideth. Updated March 24, 2024. https://www.real
simple.com/work-life/life-strategies/inspiration-motivation/habit-stacking.

Walsh, Karla. "Habit Stacking—And Why It Might Finally Help Your Behavior
Changes Stick." Everyday Health, Inc. February 13, 2023. https://www.every
dayhealth.com/emotional-health/habit-stacking-and-why-it-might-help-your-
behavior-changes-stick/.

SUPERPOWER #22: TIME MANAGEMENT

Asana, Inc. "The Eisenhower Matrix: How to Prioritize Your To-Do List." January 29, 2024. https://asana.com/resources/eisenhower-matrix.

Calm. "How to Stop Procrastinating: 9 Tips for Focus and Productivity." Accessed September 17, 2024. https://www.calm.com/blog/how-to-stop-procrastinating.

Care.com, Inc. "10 Expert-Backed Time Management Tips for Teenagers and Kids Starting Secondary School." Updated August 28, 2023. https://www.care.com/c/en-gb/time-management-tips-for-teenagers-and-kids/.

Hall, John. "Conquer Your To-Do List With the 1-3-5 Rule: A Simple Path to Productivity." Calendar. February 23, 2024. https://www.calendar.com/blog/conquer-your-to-do-list-with-the-1-3-5-rule-a-simple-path-to-productivity/.

Laurence, Emily. "What Is Procrastination? Why It Happens and How to Overcome It." *Forbes Health.* July 13, 2023. https://www.forbes.com/health/mind/procrastination/.

Maddocks, Krysten Godfrey. "Time Management Strategies: 8 Tips for Balancing College and Life." Southern New Hampshire University. May 24, 2024. https://www.snhu.edu/about-us/newsroom/education/time-management-strategies#:

MyHealth.Alberta.Ca. "Time Management for Teens: Care Instructions." Government of Alberta, Canada. Updated June 25, 2023. https://myhealth.alberta.ca/Health/aftercareinformation/pages/conditions.aspx?hwid=ug6046.

Siddhanti, Sagar. "Importance of Time Management for Teenagers." LinkedIn Corporation. May 7, 2020. https://www.linkedin.com/pulse/importance-time-management-teenagers-sagar-siddhanti.

Time Hack Hero. "Time Management for Teenagers." May 26, 2023. https://timehackhero.com/time-management-for-teenagers/.

Trengove, Deborah. "10 Tips to Help Your Teen Out of the Procrastination Trap." The Parents Website. Independent Schools Victoria. April 26, 2022. https://theparentswebsite.com.au/10-tips-to-help-your-teen-out-of-the-procrastination-trap/.

Uche, Ugo. "8 Ways to Help Your Teen to Stop Procrastinating." Psychology Today. October 13, 2022. https://www.psychologytoday.com/intl/blog/promoting-empathy-your-teen/202210/8-ways-help-your-teen-stop-procrastinating.

Vallejo, Michael. "Time Management for Teens: Challenges, Strategies, and Tips." Mental Health Center Kids. October 6, 2023. https://mentalhealthcenterkids.com/blogs/articles/time-management-for-teens.

Wikipedia. "Pomodoro Technique." Accessed September 17, 2024. https://en.wikipedia.org/wiki/Pomodoro_Technique.

SUPERPOWER #23: INFORMATION MANAGEMENT

Award Staffing. "Why It's Important to Keep Up with Trends in Your Industry." August 18, 2021. https://www.awardstaffing.com/why-its-important-to-keep-up-with-trends-in-your-industry/.

Campbell, Fiona. "What Kids and Teens Need to Know About Online Privacy." Mydoh. May 30, 2022. https://www.mydoh.ca/learn/blog/education/what-kids-and-teens-need-to-know-about-online-privacy/.

Duncan, Brooks. "How to Organize Files, Folders and Documents for Maximum Productivity." Asian Efficiency. Accessed June 1, 2024. https://www.asianeffi ciency.com/organization/organize-your-files-folders-documents/.

Get Ahead by LinkedIn News. "7 Tips to Help You Organize Your Important Documents." LinkedIn Corporation. October 13. 2022. https://www.linkedin. com/pulse/7-tips-help-you-organize-your-important-documents-.

Grossman, Amanda L. "How to Help a Teenager Get Organized (Create a Teen Life File)." Money Prodigy. Updated May 1, 2024. https://www.moneyprodigy. com/how-to-help-a-teenager-get-organized/.

Information School University of Washington. "What Is Information Management?" UW iSchool. Accessed September 17, 2024. https://ischool.uw. edu/programs/msim/what-is-information-management.

The Nemours Foundation. "Protecting Your Online Identity and Reputation." Nemours TeensHealth. Reviewed August 2022. https://kidshealth.org/en/ teens/online-id.html.

North Carolina Department of Information Technology (NCDIT). "Online Safety Tips for Teens." Accessed June 10, 2024. https://it.nc.gov/resources/online-safety-privacy/tips-guidance/online-safety-tips-teens.

Pinola, Melanie. "How to Organize Your Digital Files." Wirecutter. The New York Times. Updated March 5, 2024. https://www.nytimes.com/wirecutter/guides/ how-to-organize-your-digital-files/.

Thomas, Lawrence. "The Importance of Staying Up-To-Date with Industry Trends and Technological Advancements." From Retail to Startup. LinkedIn Corporation. March 14, 2023. https://www.linkedin.com/pulse/importance-staying-up-to-date-industry-trends-lawrence-thomas.

SUPERPOWER #24: MONEY MANAGEMENT

Bromberg. Michael. "Investing for Teens: What They Should Know." Investopedia. Dotdash Merideth. Updated April 22, 2024. https://www.investopedia.com/ investing-for-teens-7111843.

Capital One. "7 Money Management Tips to Help You Improve Your Finances."

September 19, 2024. https://www.capitalone.com/learn-grow/money-manage
ment/money-management-tips/.

Fitzsimons Credit Union. "13 Financial Literacy Games for Children and Adults.
Gamification Resources." Accessed October 12, 2024. https://www.fitzsimon
scu.com/financial-literacy-games-for-children-and-adults/.

Fontinelli, Amy. "How to Set Financial Goals for Your Future." Investopedia.
February 25, 2024. https://www.investopedia.com/articles/personal-finance/
100516/setting-financial-goals/.

Gethard, Gregory. "Stock Market Simulators: Play Your Way to Profits."
Investopedia. Updated August 25, 2021. https://www.investopedia.com/arti
cles/basics/09/stock-market-simulator.asp.

Goblin, Erin. "Investing for Teens: Everything You Need to Know." The Balance.
Dotdash Merideth. Updated on June 20, 2022. https://www.thebalancemoney.
com/investing-guide-for-teens-and-parents-4588018.

Huang, Echo, CFP. "10 Money Management Tips for Teens." LinkedIn Corp.
March 29, 2019. https://www.linkedin.com/pulse/10-money-management-
tips-teens-echo-huang-cfa-cfp-cpa/.

Investopedia. "Understanding Money: Its Properties, Types, and Uses." Updated
June 30, 2024. https://www.investopedia.com/terms/m/money.asp.

Khan Academy. "Compound Growth." Accessed October 12, 2024. https://www.
khanacademy.org/math/grade-8-math-tx/x42e41b058fcf4059:one-variable-
equations-inequalities-and/x42e41b058fcf4059:simple-and-compound-inter
est/a/compound-growth.

Set for College, LLC. "Budgeting for Teens: 21 Tips and Strategies for Success."
TheCollegePod. Accessed June 11, 2024. https://thecollegepod.com/budget
ing-for-teens/.

TeenBusiness Media, LLC. "7 Steps to Start Investing as a Teenager." TeenVestor.
Updated January 2, 2024. https://www.teenvestor.com/7steps.

White, Alexandria. "73% of Americans Rank Their Finances as the No. 1 Stress in
Life, According to New Capital One CreditWise Survey." CNBC. May 20,
2024. https://www.cnbc.com/select/73-percent-of-americans-rank-finances-
as-the-number-one-stress-in-life/.

SUPERPOWER #25: CAREER MANAGEMENT

Future North. "The Value of Networking as a Teen: 10 Ways to Make Meaningful
Connections with the Right People." November 24, 2021. https://futurenorth.
ca/the-value-of-networking-as-a-teen-10-ways-to-make-meaningful-connec
tions-with-the-right-people/.

GetAcceptd.com. "5 Tips for Teens to Make Networking Fun!" July 30, 2021. https://getacceptd.com/post/5-tips-for-teens-to-make-networking-fun.

Kamaldeep. "Importance of Setting Career Goals (and How to Do It)." Learning Routes. September 19, 2023. https://www.learningroutes.in/importance-of-setting-career-goals-and-how-to-do-it/.

The Knowledge Academy, Ltd. "Career Management: A Detailed Overview." Accessed September 17, 2024. https://www.theknowledgeacademy.com/blog/career-management/.

Martinsson, Gabrielle. "Why Setting Career Goals Is Important for You." Interviewer.AI. February 21, 2023. https://interviewer.ai/why-setting-career-goals-is-important-for-you/.

Microstartups. "Networking for Teens: The Ultimate Guide in 6+ Steps." Updated May 19, 2023. https://microstartups.org/networking-for-teens/.

WebMD, LLC. "Benefits of a Teenager Getting a Job." Reviewed April 10, 2023. https://www.webmd.com/parenting/benefits-of-a-teenager-getting-a-job.

CHAPTER 7: TECHNOLOGY AND LEARNING SKILLS

DC Extended Universe Wiki. "Cyborg." DC Extended Universe. Fandom. Accessed June 12, 2024. https://dcextendeduniverse.fandom.com/wiki/Cyborg.

Fandom. "Cyborg." Accessed October 13, 2024. https://dc-fanbase-snyderverse.fandom.com/wiki/Cyborg.

SUPERPOWER #26: NUMERACY

Cam, Daron, and Hannah Madden. "How to Improve Math Skills." WikiHow. Updated April 15, 2024. https://www.wikihow.com/Improve-Math-Skills.

CBR. "How Cyborg Became the Heart of Zach Snyder's Justice League." Accessed October 13, 2024. https://www.cbr.com/zack-snyders-justice-league-cyborg-heart-dcu/.

EduBirdie. "Mathematics and Numeracy in Everyday Life." RadioPlus Experts, LTD. February 27, 2022. https://edubirdie.com/examples/mathematics-and-numeracy-in-everyday-life/.

Latimore, Ed. "7 Ways to Improve Numeracy Skills." Stoic Street-Smarts. Accessed June 12, 2024. https://edlatimore.com/numeracy-skills/.

Prodigy. "9 Ways to Improve Math Skills Quickly & Effectively." November 1, 2021. https://www.prodigygame.com/main-en/blog/improve-math-skills/.

West, Mary. "Math Anxiety: What It Is and How to Overcome It." Medical News Today. September 29, 2022. https://www.medicalnewstoday.com/articles/math-anxiety-definition-symptoms-causes-and-tips.

SUPERPOWER #27: TECHNOLOGY SKILLS

CBR. "How Cyborg Became the Heart of Zach Snyder's Justice League." Accessed October 13, 2024. https://www.cbr.com/zack-snyders-justice-league-cyborg-heart-dcu/.

Coursera, Inc. "How Does AI Disrupt Industries?" July 24, 2024. https://www.coursera.org/articles/ai-disrupt-industry.

Coursera, Inc. "Technology Skills: What They Are and How to Improve Them." Updated June 5, 2024. https://www.coursera.org/articles/technology-skills.

Digital Hill Multimedia, Inc. "Importance of Digital Skills in Today's Workspace." Accessed June 12, 2024. https://www.digitalhill.com/blog/importance-of-digital-skills-in-todays-workplace/..

eSafety. "How to Manage Your Digital Safety Settings." Accessed September 17, 2024. https://www.esafety.gov.au/key-topics/digital-wellbeing/manage-your-digital-safety-settings.

Nebraska Library Commission. "Online Communication & Etiquette." Accessed September 25, 2024. https://nlc.nebraska.gov/Tech/literacy/communication.aspx.

SUPERPOWER #28: LEARNING SKILLS

Agboga, Victor. "10 Tips on Note-Taking in Lectures." London School of Economics and Political Science. Accessed June 14, 2024. https://info.lse.ac.uk/current-students/Assets/Articles/10-Tips-on-note-taking-during-lectures.

CBR. "How Cyborg Became the Heart of Zach Snyder's Justice League." Accessed October 13, 2024. https://www.cbr.com/zack-snyders-justice-league-cyborg-heart-dcu/.

Coursera, Inc. "11 Good Study Habits to Develop." Updated December 1, 2023. https://www.coursera.org/articles/study-habits.

Emerson, Mary Sharp. "14 Tips for Test Taking Success." Harvard Summer School. Harvard Division of Continuing Education. September 29, 2022. https://summer.harvard.edu/blog/14-tips-for-test-taking-success/.

FutureLearn. "What Is Growth Mindset and How Can You Develop One?" April 25, 2022. https://www.futurelearn.com/info/blog/general/develop-growth-mindset.

Gandi, Mustafa H., and Pinaki Makherji. "Learning Theories." National Library of Medicine. National Center for Biotechnology Information. NIH. Updated July 17, 2023. https://www.ncbi.nlm.nih.gov/books/NBK562189/.

Hreha, Jason. "What Is a Growth Mindset and How to Develop It in 9 Steps."

Persona. August 16, 2023. https://www.personatalent.com/development/how-to-cultivate-a-growth-mindset/.

Listmann, Emily. "How to Create a Study Schedule." WikiHow. February 22, 2024. https://www.wikihow.com/Create-a-Study-Schedule.

McGivney, Eileen, and Rebecca Winthrop. "Skills for a Changing World: Advancing Quality Learning for Vibrant Societies." Brookings. May 19, 2016. https://www.brookings.edu/articles/skills-for-a-changing-world/.

Wooll, "13 Tips to Develop a Growth Mindset." BetterUp. July 26, 2021. https://www.betterup.com/blog/growth-mindset.

ENDNOTES

AMBITION

1. BetterHelp, "What Does Ambition Mean? Learn About the Pursuit of Achievement."
2. CIO Views, "What Does It Mean to Have Ambition."
3. Perry, "12 Ambition Examples That'll Inspire Your Goal-Setting," BetterUp.

INTRODUCTION

1. United Nations, "Eight Trends That Will Impact Children in 2023," UN News.
2. Akkas, "Youth Suicide Risk Increased Over Past Decade," The Pew Charitable Trusts.
3. Anti-Bullying Alliance, "Prevalence of Online Bullying."
4. Davis, "Life Skills: Definition, Examples, & Skills to Build," Berkeley Well-Being Institute.
5. SkillsYouNeed, "Life Skills."
6. A-Z Quotes, "Desmond Tutu Quote."

1. HOLISTIC WELL-BEING

1. Martin, "Holistic Approaches to Well-Being and Health," Creative Healthcare Management.
2. Celebz Post, "Lessons From Batman."
3. Mayo Clinic, "Stress Management."
4. Beresin, "Stress in Teenagers," MassGeneralBrigham.
5. Cleveland Clinic, "Cortisol."
6. ReachOut.com, "Stress in Teenagers."
7. Dallas Cosmetic Dental, "10 Reasons Stress Management Matters."
8. Integris Health, "How Does Body Image Affect Mental Health?"
9. Cincinnati Children's Hospital, "Common Pressures That Can Cause Stress in Teens."
10. University of Toledo, "Deep Breathing and Relaxation."
11. Melbourne Polytechnic, "12 Ways to Manage Stress."
12. Lyness, "10 Ways to Manage Everyday Stress," Nemours TeensHealth.
13. Cincinnati Children's Hospital, "Common Pressures That Can Cause Stress in Teens."
14. gabevdesigns, "10 Effective Stress Management Techniques for Busy Professionals," Peace of Mind.

15. gabevdesigns, "10 Effective Stress Management Techniques for Busy Professionals," Peace of Mind.
16. Wikipedia, "The Dark Knight Rises."
17. Quora, "If a Professional Nutritionist Built Batman's Diet, What Would It Look Like?"
18. Pearson, "How Omega-3 Fish Oil Affects Your Brain and Mental Health," Healthline.
19. National Cancer Institute, "Antioxidants and Cancer Prevention."
20. Harvard Health Publishing, "Foods Linked to Better Brain Power."
21. Harvard Health Publishing, "Eating to Boost Energy."
22. McIntosh, "What is Serotonin, and What Does It Do?" MedicalNewsToday.
23. Harvard Health Publishing, "How to Boost Your Immune System."
24. Tinsley, "26 Foods to Eat to Gain Muscle," Healthline.
25. Mayo Clinic, "Bone Health: Tips to Keep Your Bones Healthy."
26. Neuhouser, "The Importance of Healthy Dietary Patterns in Chronic Disease Prevention," National Library of Medicine.
27. Mayo Clinic, "Dietary Fat."
28. Mayo Clinic, "Dietary Fat."
29. McIntosh, "15 Benefits of Drinking Water," *MedicalNewsToday*.
30. Johns Hopkins Medicine, "Healthy Eating During Adolescence."
31. Massachusetts General Hospital, "Have Healthy Snacks in Your Diet."
32. Mayo Clinic, "Dietary Fiber: Essential for a Healthy Diet."
33. American Heart Association, "How to Reduce Sodium in Your Diet."
34. John Muir Health, "Nutrition for Teens: Help your teenager develop a healthier relationship with food."
35. Canada's Food Guide, "Healthy Cooking Methods."
36. Gager, "Finding the Hidden Sugar in the Foods You Eat."
37. Johns Hopkins Medicine, "Healthy Eating During Adolescence."
38. Cleveland Clinic, "A Beginner's Guide to Healthy Meal Prep."
39. Gomez-Penilla, "The Influence of Exercise on Cognitive Abilities," National Library of Medicine.
40. Cox, "Role of Physical Activity for Weight Loss and Weight Maintenance," National Library of Medicine.
41. MedicinePlus, "Benefits of Exercise," National Library of Medicine.
42. MedicinePlus, "Benefits of Exercise," National Library of Medicine.
43. Hinge Health, "12 Bodyweight Exercises PTs Want You to Try."
44. Wikipedia, "High-Intensity Interval Training."
45. Centers for Disease Control and Prevention, "Youth Physical Activity Guidelines."
46. Healthi, "How to Make Physical Activity an Enjoyable Part of Your Lifestyle."
47. Mayo Clinic, "Walking: Trim Your Waistline, Improve Your Health."
48. Bryan, "Why Do We Need Sleep?" Sleep Foundation.
49. Vandekerckhove, "Emotion, Emotion Regulation, and Sleep: An Intimate Relationship," National Library of Medicine.
50. Lewis, "How Memory Replay in Sleep Boosts Creative Problem-Solving," National Library of Medicine.

51. Suni, "Mastering Sleep Hygiene: Your Path to Quality Sleep," Sleep Foundation.
52. Suni, "Teens and Sleep," Sleep Foundation.
53. Corporate Wellness Magazine, "Building a Personal Wellness Plan."
54. CHRISTUS HWC, "Mastering Wellness and Fitness."
55. Medium, "Anatomy of a Scene—The Training."
56. Perry, "Get to Know Yourself Through the Act of Self-Reflection," BetterUp.
57. Garey, "The Power of Mindfulness," Child Mind Institute.
58. Perry, "Get to Know Yourself Through the Act of Self-Reflection," BetterUp.
59. Davis, "Self-Reflection: Definition and How to Do It," The Berkeley Well-Being Institute.
60. Gupta, "The Importance of Self-Reflection," VeryWell Mind.
61. Perry, "Get to Know Yourself Through the Act of Self-Reflection," BetterUp.
62. Gupta, "The Importance of Self-Reflection," VeryWell Mind.
63. Perry, "Get to Know Yourself Through the Act of Self-Reflection," BetterUp.
64. Fandom, "Rachel Dawes," Dark Knight Wiki.
65. Physiopedia, "An Introduction to Mindfulness."
66. Cherry, "Benefits of Mindfulness," Verywell Mind.
67. Garey, "The Power of Mindfulness," Child Mind Institute.
68. Capecchi, "Mindfulness for Teens," Choosing Therapy.
69. Chemin, "5-4-3-2-1 Method."
70. Capecchi, "Mindfulness for Teens," Choosing Therapy.
71. Batts, "Men Are Still Good: An Analysis of Batman in 'Batman v Superman,'" CinemaDebate.

2. CORE PERSONAL DEVELOPMENT

1. Thompson, "Week Five—Spider-Man Learning 'With Great Power Comes Great Responsibility,'" Anchor Counseling Centers.
2. Life and Progress, "Taking Responsibility and Ownership."
3. High 5 Test, "Personal Responsibility."
4. Course Hero, "Ways on How to Become a Responsible Adolescent Prepared for Adult Life."
5. Fandom, "Peter Parker."
6. Imbastoni, "Four Steps to Create a Personal Vision Statement and Change Your Life."
7. Bell, "SMART Goals," Mind Tools.
8. Bell, "SMART Goals," Mind Tools.
9. BusinessThink, "What Are the 6 P's of Strategic Thinking," BusinessThink.
10. Asana, "What Are Smart Goals."
11. Center for Management and Organizational Effectiveness, "Strategic Thinking."
12. IMDB, "Spider-Man: Homecoming Plot."
13. White-Gibson, "Resilience in Teens," PsychCentral.
14. Mayo Clinic, "Resilience."

15. Calm, "How to Become More Resilient: 8 Ways to Build Your Resilience."
16. Barry, "'Spider-Man: Far From Home' and Seeing Beyond the Illusions," The Jesuit Post.
17. Wooll, "What is Creative Thinking and How Can I Improve?" BetterUp.
18. Newport Academy, "The Link Between Creativity and Mental Health," Teen Mental Health & Substance Abuse Treatment Centers.
19. Psychology Today, "Creativity."
20. Psychology Today, "Creativity."
21. Birt, "18 Creativity Exercises to Improve Creative Thinking at Work," Indeed.
22. Wikipedia, "Spider-Man: No Way Home."

3. ANALYTICAL AND DECISION-MAKING SKILLS

1. Marvel Cinematic Universe, "Iron Man." Fandom.
2. Wikipedia, "Iron Man."
3. Indeed, "What Are Analytical Skills? Definition, Examples and Tips."
4. Kaplan, "What Are Analytical Skills? Definition and Examples," Forage.
5. Indeed, "10 Ways to Improve Your Analytical Skills."
6. Indeed, "What Are Analytical Skills? Definition, Examples and Tips."
7. Indeed, "10 Ways to Improve Your Analytical Skills."
8. Ward, "What Is a Mind Map?" Mural.
9. IMDB, "Iron Man: Plot."
10. SessionLab, "40 Problem-Solving Techniques and Processes."
11. SkillsYouNeed, "The Best Ways to Improve Your Critical Thinking Skills."
12. Indeed, "A Guide to Critical Thinking Steps (With Benefits and Tips)."
13. Doerr, "Questioning Your Assumptions: Why It's Important for Your Personal and Professional Growth," LinkedIn.
14. University of Michigan, "Fake News and Critical Thinking in the Post-truth World."
15. Boris, "Be a Better Thinker with These 7 Critical Thinking Exercises," ABLE.
16. Handel, "Playing Devil's Advocate with Negative Beliefs," The Emotion Machine.
17. Wikipedia, "Iron Man 2."
18. Liles, "50 Lateral Thinking Puzzles That'll Stretch Your Mind in a Whole New Way," Parade.
19. Never Felt Better, "Review: Iron Man 3."
20. Herrity, "Decision-Making Skills," Indeed.
21. Han, "7 Ways to Improve Your Ethical Decision-Making," Harvard Business School Online.
22. Griffin, "How to Improve Your Decision-Making Skills," WikiHow.
23. Wikipedia, "Avengers: Endgame."

4. COMMUNICATION AND INTERPERSONAL SKILLS

1. Coursera, "What Is Effective Communications? Skills for Work, School, and Life."
2. Saavedra, "Communication Skills," Berkeley Well-Being Institute.
3. SkillsYouNeed, "Communication Skills."
4. Cleveland Clinic, "7 Ways to Improve Your Active Listening Skills."
5. Buckner, "What Is Effective Communication?" Indeed.
6. Hollander, "Average Human Attention Span by Age," Bridge Care.
7. CFI Education, "Communication Skills."
8. Cuncic, "7 Active Listening Techniques for Better Communication," Verywell Mind.
9. Segal, "Body Language and Nonverbal Communication: Communicating Without Words," HelpGuide.
10. Vyas, "Nonverbal Communication," LinkedIn.
11. Ackerman, "49 Communication Activities, Exercises, & Games," Positive Psychology.
12. Mikula, "Wonder Woman," *The Bi-College News*.
13. Coursera, "What Are Interpersonal Skills?"
14. Manson, "3 Core Components of a Healthy Relationship."
15. Reid, "Empathy," HelpGuide.
16. Marriage In A Box, "Trust and Respect Are the Key to a Healthy Relationship."
17. Poorkavoos, "Eight Behaviors That Build Trust," Roffey Park Institute.
18. SkillsYouNeed, "Interpersonal Skills."
19. Model United Nations, "Model United Nations."
20. Martines, "Wonder Woman 2017," OpenOregon.
21. The Big Red Group, "Mastering the Art of Negotiation for Teens!"
22. Dodge, "Why Your Students Need Strong Negotiating Skills," Ozobot.
23. MiddleEarth, "The Importance of Negotiation Skills for Adolescents."
24. SkillsYouNeed, "What Is Negotiation?"
25. Board Game Geek, "Negotiation Games."
26. Mikula, "Wonder Woman," *The Bi-College News*.
27. Modern Recovery, "Conflict Resolution."
28. Everyday Speech, "Promoting Harmony."
29. Vallejo, "A Guide for Conflict Resolution for Teens," Mental Health Center Kids.
30. eSoft Online Training Solutions, "Effective Guide to Conflict Resolution for Teenagers."
31. Glaser, "7 of Our Favorite Conflict Resolution Games and Activities," HRDQ.
32. Wyatt, "Wonder Woman 2017 Movie Review," Medium.

MID-BOOK REVIEW PAGE

1. Lady Spain, "Superheroes Inspirational Quotes," Oh My Fiesta! For Geeks.

5. LEADERSHIP AND TEAMWORK

1. Wallace, "10 Leadership Secrets from Captain America," Selling Power.
2. Adler, "Why Captain America Is the Leadership Role Model You Didn't Know You Needed," LinkedIn.
3. Pandey, "What Is Leadership?" Emeritus India.
4. Martins, "How to Lead by Example, According to One Asana Leader," Asana, Inc.
5. Van De Hey, "The Power of Positive Reinforcement," LinkedIn.
6. Spirit, "The 5 Steps of Leadership Process in Business," LinkedIn.
7. Martins, "How to Lead by Example," Asana.
8. The Big Red Group, "10 Ways to Develop Leadership Skills as a Teen."
9. IMDB, "Captain America: The Winter Soldier."
10. Cherry, "Emotional Intelligence," Verywell Mind.
11. Sudbrink, "Emotional Intelligence Is an Important Part of Strong Leadership," Business Leadership Today.
12. Cherry, "5 Key Emotional Intelligence Skills," Verywell Mind.
13. Moulton, "Journaling for Success: Enhancing Emotional Intelligence," LinkedIn.
14. Wikipedia, "Captain America: Civil War."
15. Perry, "What Will Make or Break Your Next Role? Find Out Why Teamwork Matters," BetterUp.
16. Perry, "What Will Make or Break Your Next Role? Find Out Why Teamwork Matters," BetterUp.
17. Perry, "What Will Make or Break Your Next Role? Find Out Why Teamwork Matters," BetterUp.
18. IMDB, "The Avengers."
19. Prakash, "Responsible Citizenship," SarvaYog.
20. Latham, "Young Volunteers: The Benefits of Community Service," University of Nevada, Reno Extension.
21. Heldt, "The Importance of Community Service in a Teen's Life," The Bridge Teen Center.
22. Prakash, "Responsible Citizenship," SarvaYog.
23. Schwartz, "50 Community Service Ideas for Teen Volunteers," TeenLife.
24. YMCA of the USA, "24 Volunteer Ideas for Teens."
25. IMDB, "Captain America: The First Avenger."
26. Wallace, "10 Leadership Secrets from Captain America," Selling Power.

6. PRACTICAL LIFE MANAGEMENT

1. Marvel Unlimited. "Natasha Romanova: Black Widow."
2. Daoire, "Habit vs. Routine." Shimmer.
3. Arlinghaus, "The Importance of Creating Habits and Routines," National Library of Medicine.
4. Arlinghaus, "The Importance of Creating Habits and Routines," National Library of Medicine.
5. Gardner, "Making Health Habitual: The Psychology of 'Habit Formation' and General Practice." National Library of Medicine.
6. Calm, "How Long Does It Take to Create a Habit (And How to Do It)?"
7. American Heart Association, "How to Break Bad Habits and Change Behaviors."
8. Cleveland Clinic, "How to Break Bad Habits."
9. Maddocks, "Time Management Strategies," Southern New Hampshire University.
10. Siddhanti, "Importance of Time Management for Teenagers," LinkedIn.
11. MyHealth.Alberta.Ca, "Time Management for Teens," Government of Alberta, Canada.
12. Asana, "The Eisenhower Matrix."
13. Asana, "The Eisenhower Matrix."
14. Hall, "Conquer Your To-Do List With the 1-3-5 Rule," Calendar.
15. Hall, "Conquer Your To-Do List With the 1-3-5 Rule," Calendar.
16. Wikipedia, "Pomodoro Technique."
17. Wikipedia, "Pomodoro Technique."
18. Calm, "How to Stop Procrastinating."
19. Laurence, "What Is Procrastination?" *Forbes Health*.
20. Trengove, "10 Tips to Help Your Teen Out of the Procrastination Trap," The Parents Website.
21. Information School University of Washington, "What Is Information Management?" UW iSchool.
22. Campbell, "What Kids and Teens Need to Know About Online Privacy," Mydoh.
23. The Nemours Foundation, "Protecting Your Online Identity and Reputation," Nemours TeensHealth.
24. North Carolina Department of Information Technology (NCDIT), "Online Safety Tips for Teens."
25. Duncan, "How to Organize Files, Folders and Documents for Maximum Productivity," Asian Efficiency.
26. Pinola, "How to Organize Your Digital Files," Wirecutter.
27. Grossman, "How to Help a Teenager Get Organized (Create a Teen Life File)," Money Prodigy.
28. Get Ahead by LinkedIn News, "7 Tips to Help You Organize Your Important Documents," LinkedIn.

29. Award Staffing, "Why It's Important to Keep Up with Trends in Your Industry."
30. Capital One, "7 Money Management Tips to Help You Improve Your Finances."
31. Goblin, "Investing for Teens," The Balance.
32. Bromberg, "Investing for Teens," Investopedia.
33. Investopedia, "Understanding Money."
34. Khan Academy, "Compound Growth."
35. Khan Academy, "Compound Growth."
36. Huang, "10 Money Management Tips for Teens," LinkedIn.
37. Set for College, "Budgeting for Teens," TheCollegePod.
38. Set for College, 'Budgeting for Teens," TheCollegePod.
39. TeenBusiness Media, "7 Steps to Start Investing as a Teenager," TeenVestor.
40. Fontinelli, "How to Set Financial Goals for Your Future," Investopedia.
41. Fitzsimons Credit Union, "13 Financial Literacy Games for Children and Adults (Gamification Resources)."
42. Gethard, "Stock Market Simulators," Investopedia.
43. The Knowledge Academy, "Career Management."
44. Martinsson, "Why Setting Career Goals Is Important for You," Interviewer.AI.
45. Microstartups, "Networking for Teens."
46. Kamaldeep, "Importance of Setting Career Goals (and How to Do It)," Learning Routes.
47. Future North, "The Value of Networking as a Teen."
48. WebMD, "Benefits of a Teenager Getting a Job."

7. TECHNOLOGY AND LEARNING SKILLS

1. DC Extended Universe Wiki, "Cyborg."
2. EduBirdie, "Mathematics and Numeracy in Everyday Life," RadioPlus Experts, LTD.
3. West, "Math Anxiety," Medical News Today.
4. Latimore, "7 Ways to Improve Numeracy Skills," Stoic Street-Smarts.
5. Latimore, "7 Ways to Improve Numeracy Skills," Stoic Street-Smarts.
6. CBR, "How Cyborg Became the Heart of Zach Snyder's Justice League."
7. Coursera, "Technology Skills: What They Are and How to Improve Them."
8. Digital Hill Multimedia, Inc. "Importance of Digital Skills in Today's Workspace."
9. eSafety, "How to Manage Your Digital Safety Settings."
10. Coursera, "How Does AI Disrupt Industries?"
11. Nebraska Library Commission, "Online Communication & Etiquette."
12. CBR, "How Cyborg Became the Heart of Zach Snyder's Justice League."
13. Gandi, "Learning Theories," National Library of Medicine.
14. McGivney, "Skills for a Changing World," Brookings.
15. FutureLearn, "What Is Growth Mindset and How Can You Develop One?"

16. Hreha, "What Is a Growth Mindset and How to Develop It in 9 Steps," Persona.
17. Coursera, "11 Good Study Habits to Develop."
18. Listmann, "How to Create a Study Schedule," WikiHow.
19. Agboga, "10 Tips on Note-Taking in Lectures," London School of Economics and Political Science.
20. Wooll, "13 Tips to Develop a Growth Mindset," BetterUp.
21. CBR, "How Cyborg Became the Heart of Zach Snyder's Justice League."
22. DC Extended Universe, Fandom, "Cyborg."

CONCLUSION

1. A-Z Quotes, "Desmond Tutu Quote."

www.ingramcontent.com/pod-product-compliance
Lightning Source LLC
Chambersburg PA
CBHW060416130626
46555CB00005B/2090